# Another Chance

*Postwar America, 1945–1968*

*R. Jackson Wilson, Editor*

# Another Chance

## Postwar America, 1945–1968

## by James Gilbert

TEMPLE UNIVERSITY PRESS 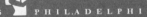 PHILADELPHIA

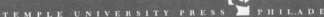

*For Jenny and Simone*

Temple University Press, Philadelphia 19122
© 1981 by Alfred A. Knopf, Inc.
Published 1981
Printed in the United States of America

Library of Congress Cataloging in Publication Data

Gilbert, James Burkhart.
  Another chance.

  Bibliography: p.
  Includes index.
    1. United States—History—1945–   . I. Title.
E741.G54   973.92   81-8916
ISBN 0-87722-224-X      AACR2

Manufactured in the United States of America

# Foreword

A foreword is a type of ritual moment—the occasion for an editor to introduce an author to the public. In some ways, this moment resembles the introductions that masters of ceremonies give to their (invariably) distinguished guests. And when we hear the staged voices of those whose role it is merely to introduce, we are skeptical. There is a false ring to it all, usually, and we are likely to doubt the sincerity of the words "an honor" or "a great personal pleasure."

Because of this, it is uncomfortable to present someone we really *do* think is distinguished, and whom it really *does* give us pleasure to introduce to an audience. It is, in fact, an honor to help bring James Gilbert's *Another Chance* to publication. It is a fine book. It confronts a difficult task with intelligence, courage, and good sense, and it performs the task with quiet modesty.

The task is to make sense out of the experience of the men, women, and children of the United States during the two decades following World War II. *Another Chance* is the history of that experience, but it is history in a sense that differs somewhat from the usual and traditional meanings of the word: *Another Chance* tries to tell a complete story. It addresses more than the doings of politicians and diplomats, generals and labor leaders. These people are in the book, but they do not control it. James Gilbert has written the story not only of the powerful and the celebrated but also of "ordinary" people. He has attempted to understand what it meant to be a child or a mother in those years—or to be old or poor. *Another Chance* is the history of a whole society. It deals with the ways Americans governed each other. But it also attempts to understand something of how they worked, entertained themselves, married and divorced, got sick, and worried about their streets, their neighborhoods, and their schools. Perhaps most of all, *Another*

*Chance* tries to understand how Americans of all kinds thought and felt about their experience.

The notion of crisis has become debased. We live from crisis to crisis. Our presidents rise and fall in crises, and, in the end, there seems to be no normality against which to measure any new crisis. But however bankrupt the rhetoric of crisis may have become for Americans of the 1980s, there can be little doubt that the generation whose experience *Another Chance* interprets did come onto the scene at the end of a long period of crisis. The Great Depression and World War II had threatened their world more severely than any event since the Civil War. And the threat had lasted longer than any other, with possibilities of defeat much more disastrous than any their ancestors had confronted. In 1945, they did seem to have another chance.

But, as James Gilbert very wisely knows, the new chance was itself fraught with the possibilities of defeat and social collapse. The ways in which Americans learned to perceive these new dangers— and the often faulty means they attempted to devise to meet them—constitute a fascinating history. And *Another Chance* presents that history with real clarity and subtlety. From its pages we come away with an enlarged, and perhaps more sympathetic, picture of what (depending on our age) we, or our parents, or our grandparents were and did.

A French philosopher once observed that those who will not learn from the errors of the past are doomed to repeat them. But French philosophers have always had an unfortunate weakness for the clever phrase, the *bon mot*. The truth is that those who do try to learn from the mistakes of the past are probably doomed to invent their own new mistakes. The decent wisdom of *Another Chance* lies in its underlying awareness that those who will not learn from the past are really doomed to be solitary—to think that their times and crises, their lonely rendezvous with their private destinies, are unique. Because he has been able to understand so much of what ordinary Americans felt and experienced a generation ago, Gilbert is able to offer us the most valuable gift of the historian: a grasp of the fact that others have been here before and have passed through their incomplete trials and triumphs with the same stubbornly inconclusive results. Herein lies the fine irony of his title: history, as long as it continues to happen, is always another chance.

This book is part of a series of studies of the History of American Society. In each book of the series, a talented young historian attempts to tell the story of experience in the United States. And, in each book, the purpose is the same: to present the history of all the people, in all its aspects, and to do so briefly, clearly, and with a minimum of scholarly jargon and apparatus. The net result, we believe, is an understanding of the national past as a whole that is as fine as the one achieved in *Another Chance*.

R.J.W.
Northampton, Massachusetts
August 1981

# Preface

Looking back at the immediate past from the perspective of the present, like viewing a length of trail just hiked over, can be disorienting. Only as we move upward and away from the narrow track of the present do its shapes take on meaning, its switch-backs become obvious, and its paths criss-cross into clear patterns. It is, of course, too soon to make definitive judgments, but some of the major turnings in the path through the tangle of contemporary events are becoming clear.

At least two distinct periods can now be distinguished since 1945: one that began in the midst of World War II and extended into the late 1960s and another rather different one since then. This book explores the first, remarkable, postwar period, although it ends with a sketch of some of the forces and energies that have emerged since 1968 and have moved politics, social life, culture, and the economy in new directions.

The most important source of energy in the postwar world was America's undeniable economic success and stability. This achievement created opportunities as well as obligations for action in world affairs. On the domestic front, it offered previously excluded minorities of the American population a wider share in prosperity and the rights of citizenship than they had ever enjoyed. By the end of the 1960s, the United States played a leading role in the revolution of rising expectations at home and abroad—a role that was as uncomfortable as it was exciting.

Extraordinary political stability and continuity during this period underscored domestic confidence that federal and bureaucratic programs could and should be used to solve social problems and reduce inequalities. At the same time, attitudes toward these problems and their solutions changed in the context of a new urban and suburban culture that predominated after the war. Counterbalanced by frequent social and economic crises, economic success and new life-styles and racial and sexual relationships accelerated the sense of change. Viewed increasingly through the new mass medium of television, culture appeared in a state of rapid and inexorable flux.

It is a challenging task to describe the economic, political, social, and cultural changes of postwar America and do justice to each. The method I have employed is thematic, attempting to demonstrate the relationship of social and cultural change to more commonly discussed subjects of economic and political trends. To this end, I have separated the chronology of presidential administrations from some of the broad social and cultural questions that preoccupied Americans during this period. I have examined these social and cultural topics at length. I have placed them, however, in such a way as to indicate their importance and relevance to political change. The result will be, I hope, a richer and broader picture of society, and one that will reflect some of the subtle tones of American culture during this period.

Many people have generously helped me in one way or another with this book, and I am delighted to acknowledge their assistance. The following persons read all or parts of the work: Herman Belz, George Callcott, Frank Freidel, William Graebner, Nelson Lichtenstein, and Larry Myers. Fellow researchers at the Library of Congress unwittingly helped me temper some of my ideas about the postwar period over lunch and coffee breaks. They include Cindy Aron, Kenneth S. Lynn, Carolyn L. Karcher, Dorothy Ross, and Jon Wakelyn.

I am especially grateful to R. Jackson Wilson, editor of the series of which this book is a part, who first persuaded me to undertake this work and then made the sorts of quiet comments that opened, and sometimes closed, the doors of speculation. Barry Karl gave me encouragement and criticism in exactly the right doses. Editors David Follmer and especially John Sturman offered suggestions. My typist Sue McLaughlin made order out of a chaos of revisions. Finally, I am deeply indebted to the libraries of various federal agencies in Washington, D.C., particularly the U.S. Army, for their help and generosity in suppying photographs.

J.G.
College Park, Maryland
August 1981

# Contents

# *Another Chance*

*Postwar America, 1945–1968*

# Prologue
# Rising Expectations

In September 1945, *Look* magazine published a photographic essay picturing the distinctive features of American society. Stressing an old theme, the essay disparaged the notion that "the frontier is gone." How foolish to dwell on limitations, it continued, when possibilities opened everywhere. "Here is a partial list of America's new frontiers," it concluded: "the modern house . . . the automatic washer . . . express highways . . . television . . . the private plane . . . quick freezing." Fifteen years later, in his campaign for the presidency, John Kennedy invoked the same idiom of expansion and promise, although he certainly had more in mind than *Look*'s shopping list. If anything, the sense of potential had deepened during the intervening years. Millions of Americans agreed with Kennedy; the decades following years of depression and war had renewed interrupted dreams and added new ambitions. As the *Reader's Digest* predicted in 1945, these were years when Americans had a precious "chance to make a second start."

People in every age probably think of themselves as exceptional—singular in their wisdom and experience and unique in the opportunities they have seized, the risks they have run. Certainly, postwar Americans portrayed themselves in this fashion. This generation took suburban living as its ideal at home and the Cold War as its ideology in foreign policy. It engendered a baby boom and then lived through a youth rebellion, but it was very much shaped by the heritage of the Depression of the 1930s and the unfinished business of World War II. In the marriage of existing American culture to the new world of 1945, the mass media, shifting sexual practices and family arrangements, mobility, and population and political changes were both old and new, with deep roots in the past. Yet, for all the persistence of past problems, the postwar world, more than any previous age, seemed to fulfill ideals of American exceptionalism and the American dream.

Age-old problems in race relations and poverty appeared just at the point of solution. The economy no longer rose and plunged in twenty-year waves of calm and storm. Emancipation from customary practices in culture and social life, so fervently predicted since the 1920s, now seemed real. Dread communicable diseases and the maladies of deprivation and malnutrition expired. Liberation, affluence, and technological progress made optimism the natural creed of many Americans.

The reasons for this optimism lie partly in the way the war ended. The United States emerged with the world at its feet. Power accumulated as the nation accelerated its economic and political penetration of developed and underdeveloped societies. In the relative vacuum left by the destruction of Europe, the expansion of the American economic system through links to raw materials producers and markets drew the United States into internationalism on an unprecedented scale. Thereafter, changing definitions of what counted in American survival focused the nation's attention on once obscure and remote places in Asia, Eastern Europe, and South America. The United States became the dominant nation on the planet.

More closely and rationally guided than ever before, the American economy achieved a remarkable height of production and breadth of distribution. Reform programs, social security, and, eventually, in the mid-1960s, subsidized medical care for the elderly softened inequalities and strengthened the purchasing power of all Americans, while contributing a critical element to the gross national product. As the economy shifted to services and consumer jobs, with less blue-collar work, more federal and state regulation, automation of the workplace, and expansion of credit-dependent family economies, Americans redefined their necessities to include what other ages had thought to be luxuries.

During the postwar years, and especially after 1960, American life-styles changed rapidly; indeed, the very term "life-style" signified the fluidity of social mores. The family structure shifted and relaxed. The decline of censorship and the impact of advertising, television, and other media made even private sexual fantasies the subject of mass culture. Toleration for once-repressed sexual practices, for new marital arrangements, for experiments in drug use changed the overt beliefs of many Americans. More importantly, shifts in the attitudes of women, blacks, and other minorities toward their own rights, and the general acceptance of these claims by the rest of society, allowed a minority of black Americans to enter the middle strata of employment and freed the vast majority from restrictions that had bound them since the beginning of the century. For women, equal pay for equal work became more commonplace.

Politically, these were years of Democratic party hegemony. The ideas, innovations, and coalitions that blossomed out of the arid ground of the 1930s returned, perennially, to ornament the political landscape of the 1950s and 1960s. Despite the interim of Republican presidencies, 1953–1960 and 1969–1976, the fundamental consensus of American politics derived from the practices of executive leadership, federal regulation, and interest-group coalitions developed by the Democratic leadership in the 1930s and 1940s. Even when out of national office, the Democratic party maintained its leading edge in politics by dominating Congress and a majority of state governments.

Viewed from the perspective of 1981, the years from 1945 to the end of the 1960s deserve recognition for their coherence as a period and for their social achievements. Even in the darkest years of the war in Vietnam, when the shouts of critics were loudest, the most ardent dissenters shaped their vision of the good society out of promises made in the recent past.

These almost tangible possibilities of harmony and success certainly did not die in the 1970s, but they did revert to the more familiar—and abstract—guise of aspirations and visions. Suddenly, problems that had existed, albeit obscurely, reemerged with force. The war in Vietnam, the riots in American cities, the weakening of presidential leadership and political parties exposed the underlying limitation of resources and the narrowness of consensus that optimism had once masked. From the time of the second Eisenhower administration in the 1950s, the terrain under American interests and alliances abroad began to shift. As the Soviet Union, Western Europe, and Japan rebuilt and modernized their economies and underdeveloped countries increasingly husbanded their natural resources, the United States saw its relative economic and political power shrink. By the 1970s, competition for markets and raw materials and the diffusion of technology and production created a world in which the United States was preponderant but not unique.

Just as striking was the transformation of American politics. After the election of 1968, political parties had increasing difficulty translating the contradictions of American society into national compromises. The existence of discredited and unpopular leaders in both parties coincided with a decline in shared goals. The growing importance of the media and political polling, on the one hand, emphasized narrowly defined and free-floating single-issue groups and, on the other, contributed to growing apathy and a feeling of remoteness in voters. Ironically, expansion of the means of communication eroded trust in the ability to communicate.

Victories in social reform, as some observers had warned, did not always break the tenacious grasp of old intolerances. The advances and successes in the struggle for equality for all Americans relaxed but could not release the hold of racism and sexism in society. Backlash, timidity, class conflict, as well as deep-seated custom and belief pushed the struggle for equality to a more complex plane. Abolition of segregation did not necessarily mean integration. Sex-divided job opportunities still existed despite the number of working women. For every wrong corrected, a new puzzle had to be solved, with the rights of others to be adjusted.

During the 1970s, the divisions in society attracted increasing attention. Americans, more conscious of limitations, soberly appraised their society. The focus on conflict and the insistent demands of the most vocal components of society suggested a nation defined by its peripheral elements and not by its center—the parts never adding up to the whole. It suggested a society divided about goals and uncertain about its future. Nothing in this state of affairs could be more distinct from the period of the first years following World War II, when the course still seemed clear: a generation about to embark on fulfilling its dreams and a nation about to be given a second chance after a decade of depression and four years of war.

# 1 Shaping the Things To Come

Sitting by the fireside of his Little White House retreat on Pine Mountain, Georgia on April 12, 1945, President Franklin D. Roosevelt suddenly complained of a terrible headache. Shortly afterward, doctors pronounced him dead. Two hours later, the new President, Harry S Truman, swore the oath of office in Washington. For many Americans, it was hard to imagine a presidency without Roosevelt; he had presided over seven years of depression and five years of war. Hundreds of thousands of citizens lined the streets to watch his funeral cortege pass from Union Station to the White House. A young Texas representative, Lyndon Baines Johnson, interviewed by *The New York Times*, poignantly expressed his anguish: "I don't know that I'd ever have come to Congress if it hadn't been for him." He frankly wondered what would happen without F.D.R. "There are plenty of us left to try to block and run interference, as he had taught us, but the man who carried the ball is gone—gone." Others wondered too. In the Soviet Union, newspapers broke their tradition against placing foreign news on the first page, running a front-page, black-edged photograph of Roosevelt and editorials praising the leader of the nation's staunch ally.

In the springtime of 1945, the United States stood at the threshold of a great military victory. Victory, however, was a fragile trophy in a desperate and turbulent world. Beyond its own shores, America looked over a shattered and disorderly world. The major European powers—even the victors—had lost heavily in casualties, economic facilities, and military hardware. The Soviet Union sustained an awesome 22 to 24 million dead in the war; Germany lost 4.2 million. While France and Italy suffered relatively few casualties, the experience of Fascist regimes in both countries discredited old political institutions and former leaders. Each country emerged from the war in political and emotional confusion; each was torn by elements that supported or opposed a serious economic and political restructuring of its society along socialist lines. Disarray and weakness in the old European colonial powers aided African and Asian nationalists who sought to destroy colonial regimes and build their own independent nation-states.

In this disorderly world, the United States was the exception. Victory represented a triumph of order, planning, and production, not just an expenditure of blood. A Gallup poll, published in early 1945, confirmed this judgment. Only 36 percent of Americans represented admitted that they had made any real sacrifice for the war; and most of this minority mentioned the absence or death of a relative in the armed forces. The great majority replied that they felt no great loss or deprivation.

Despite extravagance, waste, and corruption, America's gross national product increased dramatically, from about $91 billion in 1939 to about $212 billion in 1945. Even the economic and social effects of fielding a huge army while increasing production were contained. Mobilization of a large army meant the transportation, training, and housing of millions of young men away from home. Their withdrawal from factories and farms left jobs to be filled by women, Southern blacks, and retired or very young workers. In general, this shift to a new working population occurred smoothly; federal institutions, like the War Manpower Commission, worked with local governments and industry to recruit and accommodate workers and ease their special problems.

There were many serious disagreements about what to do in the future, but few observers could deny that centralized control, social planning, and massive government stimulation of the economy had pulled the nation out of the Depression of the 1930s. This success, however, raised more questions than it settled. World War II generated a great social and economic experiment but not everyone agreed on the lessons that had been learned. More importantly, because of its enormous financial power, the federal government affected every aspect of the economy—even when it refused to act. No one could ignore its future role.

Lack of comprehensive planning worried such figures as Henry Wallace, Vice-President (until 1944) and *bête noire* of conservative Democrats, but a favorite of liberal and labor segments in the Roosevelt political coalition. In his widely read book *The Century of the Common Man* (1943) Wallace wrote that American exceptionalism (the exemption from European-style social revolution) would not last beyond the end of the war. Without "vigorous" government actions, he said, a wave of economic storms would sweep the country: inflation, scarcities, bankruptcy, and possibly "violent revolution." Sounding very much as if he were describing conditions during the Great Depression of the 1930s, Wallace was only dramatizing fears shared by many economists, sociologists, and political leaders of the day.

Writing for a conference held in New York on the Scientific Spirit and Democratic Faith, philosopher Jerome Nathanson expressed a more common opinion about planning: "The chief problem of our time is how to plan our economic and social life without sacrificing freedom." This proposition was no mere rhetorical flourish. It went straight to the core of American hesitations about the role of state intervention. Most Americans in 1945 firmly believed in the inevitable antagonism between individualism and democracy, on the one hand, and planning and state activity on the other. The Depression and then the war temporarily suspended this belief, but it remained an overarching assumption.

The experience of the 1930s shaped the anticipations and actions of Americans in all walks of life. Although many people were untouched by the ravages of the Depression, it formed the central feature of the decade's topography. Economic insecurity, breadlines, Hoovervilles, and make-work relief hovered as uncomfortable memories. As late as 1939, official unemployment figures had been extremely high: 9 million or 17 percent of the work force. The Depression had broader effects than such statistics reveal; it disrupted the educational, marital, and child-rearing plans of many young Americans; it abruptly ended careers and forced many ablebodied men and women to question their own abilities and dignity; and it focused both culture and art upon those persistent elements of solidarity and community in the American experience. Most Americans emerged from the Depression with more, not less, faith in traditional institutions like the family. Security, not experimentation, was their aim. Thus a *Fortune* magazine survey of workers taken in 1943 found surprisingly few who would risk job security for an uncertain reward or advancement. Fifty-five percent preferred to keep a low-paying secure job. Only a few would opt for very high pay if the chances of failure were also great. Perhaps as educator James B. Conant wrote in 1940, the experience of the 1930s had shattered "the modern soul" and lowered expectations about the ability of industrial society to bring happiness to its citizens.

Few significant politicians—certainly not Roosevelt—advocated comprehensive government guidance of the economy. Most policymakers, economists, businessmen, and labor unions recognized that some forms of governmental interference in the economy were beneficial and in their own interests. But, they were unsure how far to go in the direction of federal planning. They did not agree about who should do the planning or who should benefit from social programs initiated by the state. Inevitably, government programs that emerged from the war were sometimes contradictory—shocking in their limitations or unprecedentedly generous in their comprehensiveness.

During the war, the federal government established one major planning organization, housed in the executive branch. It had a brief and controversial existence, however. First formed in 1933 as the National Planning Board, F.D.R. reorganized it as the National Resources Planning Board (NRPB) in 1939. Headed by F.D.R.'s uncle, Frederic Delano, the board began comprehensive discussions of the role of government in the postwar economy. In reports, conferences, and interdepartmental policy dinners, members of the Washington board discussed plans for demobilization, public services, social security, and financial and fiscal problems. Their overriding concern was unemployment. On this delicate issue, the Trends and Stabilization Section, directed by economist Paul A. Samuelson, suggested federal action to achieve full employment after the war. Other activities of the NRPB included regional planning conferences for demobilization and reconversion to peacetime production. Preliminary plans were drawn up for such regions as the "Niagara Frontier," Denver Metropolitan area, and the Puget Sound area.

Perhaps the most controversial proposal of the NRPB was its National Production and Employment Budget. This alternative budget was designed to be countercyclical, that is, it had built-in government spending and fiscal management elements triggered to work against the business cycle in order to prevent recessions or runaway booms. Its goal was full employment, but critics could only see it as a flagrant step toward socialism.

While F.D.R. may have approved some of the NRPB's goals, he would not fight to keep it in existence. When Congress voted to eliminate funds for the board in 1943, it rejected not just this body, but the only effective executive branch planning organization. Perhaps this was inevitable, for whatever Roosevelt's sympathies for the NRPB's work, his own style of administration was very different. Where he preferred to improvise and divide authority, planners hoped to anticipate and centralize.

The major bureaucratic agency of economic control during the war was the Office of War Mobilization, created in May 1943 and transformed into the Office of War Mobilization and Reconversion (OWMR) in October 1944. Headed by James F. Byrnes, this superagency coordinated manpower, production, and resource allocation and supervised specific federal agencies concerned directly with the economic war effort. As a central planning bureau, the OWMR might have formed the nucleus for postwar economic coordination, but there was no move to transfer its functions to peacetime. In fact, the major controversy inside the agency related to how quickly the United States economy should be allowed to convert to civilian production. After 1943, several important figures, led by Donald M. Nelson, the chairman of the War Production Board, fought with some success to begin peacetime conversion. From 1943 to August 1944, limited reconversion was allowed in consumer industries, but the serious reverses of the Battle of the Bulge in Belgium during that summer ended this limited experiment. Military planners who demanded full production of war material until the end of the war prevailed. Thus, when the OWMR disbanded in December 1946, no one thought to continue it as an economic planning agency.

Roosevelt's most fully articulated plans for postwar society suggest that he agreed with the goal of a speedy reconversion to private ownership and production and a dismantling of controls. In early 1944, the administration approved the Baruch Plan for Demobilization and Industry Reconversion. Drawn up by industrialist Bernard Baruch, head of the War and Postwar Adjustment Advisory Unit of the War Mobilization Board, the plans dictated speedy termination of government war contracts and quick reconversion to civilian production. They set up standard guidelines to facilitate rapid conversion to consumer production. Removal of price controls and limitations on scarce materials were deferred to the end of the conflict. Nonetheless, it is clear that Roosevelt intended to return the economic initiative to private business as soon as possible.

Congress made one last effort in 1946 to institute some form of federal planning in the Full Employment Bill. Debated in the midst of acrimonious strikes and intensifying difficulties abroad, the bill was eventually gutted of its mandatory investment features. When signed on February 20, 1946 by President Truman, the law had a less ambitious title, the Employment Law. It dropped specific reference to a National Production and Employment Budget, but it did commit the federal government to the goal of full employment, and it established a Presidential Council of Economic Advisers and a Congressional Joint Committee on the Economic Report. It required the President in conjunction with the advisers to issue an annual report on the economy. Thus, it retained the outlines of planning without specific powers. The federal government committed itself in theory to intervene actively in the economy, but that commitment remained fuzzy, ill-defined, and controversial.

This did not mean that the federal government took no role in the economy; on the contrary, its power grew throughout the next three decades. And an increasing number of key government advisers and economists accepted the basic tenets of Keynesian economics (named after the British economist John Maynard Keynes). Keynes had argued that in order to control growth and prevent depressions, the national government should intervene in the economy to maintain total demand for goods and services. Through taxation and deficit spending, the government could encourage overall investment or it could dampen growth.

Despite congressional conservatism on the issue of comprehensive planning, Capitol Hill anticipated increased federal economic activity after the war. In the spring of 1943, the Senate considered several bills to prepare demobilization and postwar economic plans. An initiative proposed by Senator Walter F. George, of Georgia, passed the Senate in March 1943, establishing a Special Committee on Postwar Economic Policy and Planning.

Chaired by George, the committee investigated a number of anticipated postwar problems, such as troop demobilization, reconversion of war production, unemployment, highway development, postwar taxation, and housing and urban redevelopment. One of its most far-reaching suggestions came from its special housing subcommittee chaired by the conservative Republican Senator Robert A. Taft. Taft, working with the Banking, Education, and Labor Committees of the Senate, held hearings from June 1944 to February 1945, in which he called for a national commitment to good housing as "essential to a sound and stable democracy." Taft and his committee proposed federal commitment to slum clearance and rehousing. At least 6 million new housing units were required, and some of them would have to be public housing.

Thus the Senate, in such hearings, prefigured several of the important social and economic programs undertaken later during the Truman administration.

One major reason for federal inertia in postwar economic planning was the attitude of organized labor and business groups. Organized labor was surprisingly quiet on the issues of postwar planning. Although congressional friends of labor often stood in the forefront of planning efforts, neither the AF of L nor the CIO evidenced much direct interest in the issue until 1943. By then, the AF of L had appointed a special postwar planning committee headed by Matthew Woll; the CIO was still, at this late date, only preparing to establish such a committee. Both committees did suggest minimal national planning, but the real interests of unions lay elsewhere. Labor preferred to preserve the gains made in collective bargaining and membership under the New Deal and especially during the war, rather than to embark on ambitious new programs.

American businessmen had mixed feelings about postwar planning. While business leaders adopted important internal measures of corporate planning largely unknown before the war (General Electric, for example, directed each of its departments to plan future employment and production needs), business leaders continued to be hostile to most federal planning. Business wished to anticipate future needs, and it was willing to let government take steps to protect the economy, but, by and large, its attitudes toward central planning were antagonistic.

During 1942 and 1943, in conferences, articles, and speeches, business leaders focused on postwar problems. The most pressing of these, they urged, would be dismantling government ownership and direction of war production, elimination of controls, prevention of unemployment, and reconversion. The National Association of Manufacturers (NAM), one of the most powerful American business organizations, held two War Congresses of American Industry in 1942 and 1943. At the first of these, it adopted a War Program of American Industry, outlining wartime goals and establishing a kind of Atlantic Charter for American business. Among its several points, the NAM proposed something for every class: a prosperous agriculture, employment in free enterprise for all who could work, a higher standard of living, and the right of small operators to go into business for themselves. The principal axiom, however, was undoubtedly the second, pledging salaries and profits to all "commensurate with their performance and usefulness to society." The NAM, in other words, promised a more efficient and better operating private economy.

At the same conference, Henry J. Kaiser, president of the Kaiser Aluminum Company, outlined social goals for American industry once the war ended. He estimated that 9 million new housing units would be required immediately after the war. To meet an anticipated increase in automobile transportation, he argued for a huge new highway system. Finally, he urged private business to help promote adequate medical care for every citizen. To achieve these goals, he suggested that automakers prepare 1945 models, that construction lobbyists begin a crusade for a modern "turnpike" system, and that the medical profession push private insurance systems to head off state or socialized medicine.

Kaiser's remarks suggest the degree to which business had successfully adopted market research and planning. The astute discussions sponsored by the NAM in 1942 and 1943 reveal foresight about the shape of postwar society and accuracy in identifying the leading sectors of development—highways, automobiles, housing and health care—that would fuel the postwar boom. Other organizations, like the American Chamber of Commerce, cautiously predicted a postwar boom once controls were abandoned. In 1943, the Chamber of Commerce urged industry to plan for investment and production so that both industry and government could avoid the disastrous rollercoaster boom and depression following World War I. Pent-up demand, availability of investment capital, and conversion to the use of new materials in manufacture would prevent economic dislocations.

☆                    ☆                    ☆

Beyond organizing and directing the wartime economy, the federal government profoundly affected the lives and salaries of millions of Americans. Federal policy had its greatest postwar impact on Americans in the labor force rather than on the direction of the economy. The draft of millions of soldiers in an economy reaching full production seriously depleted the white, male industrial working class. By necessity, federal policy altered the makeup of the industrial labor force and touched off a massive migration of families from South to North, from East to West, and from rural areas to cities. As with the issue of economic planning, the *fait accompli* of wartime labor policy became the center of controversy:

Could the changes of the war be undone? To what extent, after the war, should returning soldiers be given their old positions or preference in new places? What should be done with the millions of new black and female workers? In this area, federal policy, while it ignored some serious problems, underwent extensive discussion. Never before or since has the government intervened so seriously and successfully in the lives of Americans.

Recruiting women workers on the "Home Front" was a major task undertaken by the federal government. Campaigns directed at women urged them into new and high-paying jobs in shipbuilding and aircraft and munitions manufacture. Women answered the call of patriotic duty and the lure of high wages. Approximately 5 million new women workers joined the labor force from 1941 to 1945. By 1942, about one of every three workers was female; during the next year, the figure rose to 36 percent. Women chose various sorts of work, from the "Woman's Land Army," organized to replace depleted farm labor, to defense work. By 1944, 1.25 million or about one-half of all employees in the aircraft industry were women. A good many of them labored at the intricate work of assembling B-29 bombers, the mainstay of the U.S. Air Force. Others took up welding and metallurgical work in shipbuilding. Black women, in particular, were concentrated in the ordnance industry, making small arms and ammunition. As a pamphlet published by the War Department summarized: "A woman is a substitute—like plastic instead of a metal. She has special characteristics that lend themselves to new and sometimes to such superior uses."

By the end of the war, many women refused to see themselves as substitutes. In 1946, a survey by the Federal Women's Bureau of women workers in ten major war production areas revealed that most female workers hoped to stay on the job, even after the troops came home. About 75 percent of the interviewees intended to continue working, and, of these, about 86 percent wanted to retain their current positions. They had made an indelible mark on the workplace, and only a concentrated drive could eliminate them. Factory buildings had been altered to accommodate women workers: extra restroom facilities, cafeterias, lightweight machine tools, and other special equipment, including plastic jigs, long-handled levers, and weight-lifting devices, had been adopted. In local communities, over 3,000 child-care centers were established to supervise the children of working women.

The massive entrance of women into industrial employment and

*A Symington-Gould sand slinger at rest, Buffalo, New York, May 1943. Because of the serious labor shortage during the war, women moved into nontraditional jobs in heavy industry and manufacturing, where they found higher wages and often gained new self-confidence and independence.    (Library of Congress, photo by Marjorie Collins)*

the positive publicity given to their efforts had other effects out-side the factory. For one thing, their presence created a highly skilled labor pool: over 2 million women enrolled in some form of vocational training during the war. The public commitment to "womanpower" also raised broader issues of women's rights. Equality of pay and working conditions did not always accompany women into the workplace. Unions like the AF of L enlisted new women members "for the duration only." Some locals even kept separate seniority lists for men and women. Hostility between male and female workers sometimes flared, particularly when the latter first entered an industry. Some companies, like General Electric and Westinghouse, established "women's rates" that pegged pay below the prevailing wage for males doing the same work.

Unequal treatment led to a campaign to secure justice for women. The Republicans in 1940 and the Democrats in 1944 supported an Equal Rights Amendment to the Constitution in their campaign platforms, but support lagged in two important quarters. Both the CIO and the AF of L opposed such an amendment, and the two most powerful female political figures, Eleanor Roosevelt and Frances Perkins, the Secretary of Labor, refused to support it.

On another front, strong support developed in 1945 to empower the Federal Women's Bureau to investigate sex discrimination in employment. This suggested "Federal Wage Discrimination Act" of 1945, introduced by Senator Wayne Morse, of Oregon, and Senator Claude Pepper, of Florida, enjoyed substantial backing from women's groups, the CIO, and even the conservative Republican Senator Robert A. Taft, of Ohio. The proposed act, which tried to balance the interests of women and the "reemployment rights of returned veterans," failed to pass. Although the War Labor Board issued guidelines for equal pay for equal work in 1945, the failures of the Equal Rights Amendment and the Wage Discrimination Act were handwriting on the shop wall for women employees.

By the last months of the war, Secretary of Labor Perkins seemed more worried about potential GI unemployment than the rights of women workers. She suggested that workers over sixty-five and under twenty be encouraged to retire and that women who entered the job market only because of the war should leave the work force voluntarily. The War Manpower Commission assumed that women would retire, proposing that "the separation of women from industry should follow an orderly plan." At the same time, the Commission warned employers that some women needed work. William H. Stead, the Dean of the Washington University Business School, expressed what was probably a more typical viewpoint. The major postwar employment problem, he wrote, would be to get rid of temporary workers. If two-thirds of them were removed, it would be a "tremendous" achievement.

Black workers constituted another group viewed as temporary, and therefore a problem for postwar conversion. The discriminations and restrictions faced by black workers were both similar to and different from those of white women. As in World War I, employment opportunities and labor shortages in the industrial areas of the North and West compelled a strong migration of black men and women from the South. Their movement was not accomplished without bitterness and dispute. Finding large areas of employment closed and extensive wage and skills discrimination on the job, black leaders challenged the Roosevelt administration in early 1941 to act to ensure fair treatment. A. Philip Randolph, head of the Brotherhood of Sleeping Car Porters, a powerful black trade union, and Walter White of the NAACP, threatened a demonstration in Washington to highlight the plight of black workers. In the face of this potential embarrassment, President Roosevelt issued Executive Order #8802 on June 25, 1941, creating a Fair Employment Practices Committee (FEPC) designed to enforce the pledges of equal treatment given in the Executive Order. Henceforth, any company engaged in defense production would be required to hire without regard to race, creed, color, or national origin.

Roosevelt's initiative had immediate effect. In September 1941, Lockheed Aircraft, which employed 40,000 workers, hired its first black employees. Black workers, hearing of opportunities, streamed northward to cities like Chicago and Detroit, where in some cases they had been actively recruited by the federal government. In Detroit, trouble broke out between white and black defense workers. Acrimony turned to riot in early 1942 with white opposition to black occupancy of a specially constructed housing development. Occasional wildcat strikes erupted, until, in June 1943, isolated incidents burst into a full-scale race war. In three days of battle, thirty-four persons died, hundreds were injured, until federal troops restored order. In August of the same year, frustrations again boiled over into violence, this time in Harlem. After a day of rioting, six persons had died and over 300 were injured in an angry protest over poor living conditions and the slow progress in racial equality.

Incidents such as these, plus the rumored existence of "Eleanor Clubs," named after Eleanor Roosevelt and purported to be groups of black domestics planning to strike the kitchens of white employers, persuaded F.D.R. to consider further actions to defuse racial tension. He explored, then rejected, the creation of a Commission on Race Relations. Thus, the most strenuous wartime activity on behalf of blacks remained the FEPC. And even this body was attacked in Congress in 1944. By the end of the war, with Roosevelt dead, the new President, Truman, issued Executive Order #9664 on December 20, 1945, which removed the power of the FEPC and transformed it into an advisory body. It was finally dissolved in June 1946.

This faltering federal commitment to the rights of black Americans came at a particularly difficult time for them. Returning black GIs demanded the right to vote in the deep-South states of Mississippi, Alabama, and Georgia, where a variety of legal subterfuges deprived them of the suffrage. Racial tension after demobilization increased rapidly, and white backlash precipitated local revivals of the Ku Klux Klan. Incidents abounded, particularly one in Columbia, Tennessee, where the Klan, with the complicity of local law enforcement officials, terrorized the local black community. When the smoke cleared, twenty-eight blacks had been arrested and two killed.

Incidents such as these led to the creation of the National Emergency Committee Against Mob Violence headed by Eleanor Roosevelt and Dr. Channing Tobias. Pressure from this group, plus loss of control of Congress to the Republicans in November 1946, convinced President Truman to act. On December 5, 1946, under executive order, he created a Presidential Civil Rights Committee designed to explore the problems of black Americans and to suggest remedial legislative programs. Like many other pressing internal social problems, the need to correct century-long injustices to black Americans got caught in the whirligig of demobilization. Such problems took second place to presidential and congressional preoccupation with dismantling regulations and controls over the private economy. Only when political pressure built up to the bursting point did significant action occur.

One group, however, emerged from the war with a grant of privileges and advantages practically unheard of in American history. In its case, federal planning was extensive, comprehensive, and favorable. Memories of the Depression and the troubled demobilization of 1919 focused attention on returning GIs. The American government had traditionally rewarded soldiers with cash bonuses, and sentiment ran strongly in favor of some monetary reward for World War II veterans. Many Americans felt that the sacrifice of several years' service placed returning soldiers in a poor competitive position: they had lost seniority on the job and missed crucial years in school or apprenticeship training. Possibilities of renewed depression added further worries. If returning GIs attempted to reenter the labor market simultaneously, the United States risked massive unemployment.

Planning for a GI bill was foreshadowed in the Selective Service Act of 1940, which contained a reemployment provision committing the federal government to aid returning soldiers seeking employment. Administration planners quickly realized the immensity of this commitment. They estimated that by 1945, about one-quarter of the work force would be demobilized veterans. Pressure to pass what became the Servicemen's Readjustment Act came from many quarters. More than 600 bills relating to returning GIs were introduced into the Congress during the war years. Citizen groups, particularly the American Legion, organized support for liberal grants of financial and educational benefits.

Roosevelt lent his support to this aspect of planning for the future. At first, he turned to the National Resources Planning Board to direct work on a GI bill. This body, in turn, set up a Postwar Manpower Conference incorporating representatives from educational, defense, and organized labor establishments. Their resulting recommendations favored subsidized education to compensate for time spent in the armed forces. Written with the aim of preventing postwar unemployment, the conference report revealed both the worries and the expectations of the Roosevelt administration.

At the same time, Roosevelt also created an Armed Forces Committee on Postwar Educational Opportunities, known as the Osborn Committee, after its chairman Brigadier General Frederick H. Osborn. This committee, consisting also of General Lewis Hershey of the Selective Service, of officials from the army, navy, and U.S. Office of Education, and of leading educators, published recommendations in 1943 that became the basis for the administration's bill, introduced in November by Senator Elbert

Thomas, of Utah. After a good deal of debate and effective lobbying for increased benefits by the American Legion, the Servicemen's Readjustment Act, also known as the Veterans Act or the GI
Bill, was passed and signed into law on June 22, 1944.

The Veterans Act worked a revolution in American society that
became increasingly obvious with the passage of time. Its effects
were probably unanticipated, but GI educational grants, home and
business loans, and employment preferences touched off the immense expansion of higher education that followed the war, helped
to subsidize the building of suburbia, and aided thousands of
young men in local and federal government careers. The GI Bill
encouraged a generation to view privilege as its right, giving returning soldiers a competitive edge in education and employment
that deeply affected the relative status of women and black Americans. Their advantage operated for two crucial reasons. While a
few hundred thousand women in the armed services were eligible
to use veterans' privileges, this number represented only a tiny
percentage of American women. The opportunities for returning
black GIs were theoretically more favorable, but in practice, black
GIs had restricted opportunities because of continued segregation
in private and state-funded colleges and universities, discrimination in state and federal hiring, and limited access to VA-approved
housing because of restricted covenants widely adhered to by real
estate interests and enforced by the courts during the 1940s.

The rationale for the World War II GI Bill registered worries
about potential depression, but its generous provisions indicate
the popularity of World War II. (The Korean War GI Bill and the
Cold War GI Bill were far less generous.) The best publicized
portion of the act, Title 2, dealt with higher education. Originally,
the law provided that veterans under twenty-five at the day of
entry into military service, who remained for ninety days or more,
would receive one year's subsidized education. Two years' service
earned three years of schooling. All tuition fees would be paid to
the college chosen by the veteran, plus a monthly subsistence of
$50 for single and $75 for married GIs.

Although some educators from elite universities like Harvard
and the University of Chicago worried over the potential harm
of admitting a flood of returning soldiers, most colleges and universities welcomed the additional enrollment and financing brought
by their new students. Pressure on better public institutions
mounted; Rutgers University in New Jersey, for example, enrolled

more than twice as many students (many of them GIs) in 1948 as in 1939. New York, lacking a comprehensive state educational system, suffered serious overcrowding. In 1945, Republican Governor Thomas E. Dewey and the Democratic party both advocated a new university system. The resulting system—the State University of New York (SUNY)—developed after 1948 into one of the largest, most extensive, and well-funded systems of undergraduate, graduate, and professional training in the nation. By 1947–1948, the Veterans Administration was paying the bills for almost 50 percent of the male students in institutions of higher learning. In all, some 2,232,000 veterans attended college under the first GI Bill.

Returning soldiers, who traded in their uniforms for an academic mortarboard, changed campus life. As an older generation of students, almost half of them were married. Housing was a severe problem and temporary "vetsvilles" mushroomed around state universities. In these communities, veterans developed a subculture of food co-ops, nursery schools, and wives' organizations. For the returning soldier, classroom offerings were often inappropriate; worse still, in loco parentis rules designating dating customs, hours outside dormitories, and dress codes seemed onerous or silly. As a result, many schools revised curriculum offerings and eliminated some of the more restrictive social codes.

Despite inevitable cases of graft and inefficiency, the educational provisions of the GI Bill were a huge success. Thousands of young men, who might otherwise have settled immediately into industrial jobs, attended colleges and universities. Beyond the expectations of most experts, GIs did well in schools, thereby adding to those forces pushing for democratization and expansion of higher education. Federal largesse to universities became a major staple in educational planning. By 1962, because of the additional Korean GI Bill passed in 1952, colleges and universities had received over 5 billion dollars in tuition contributions, and veterans had received over 10 billion in subsistence allowances. Simultaneous grants from state programs for veterans enlarged the opportunities of the returning GIs. State governments, such as that of Wisconsin, replicated federal spending in providing additional scholarships and subsistence programs for vets.

Part of the Servicemen's Readjustment Act set up a GI loan system. Administered by the Veterans Administration, a large fund was available to GIs for mortgage and business loan credits.

With little or no down payment, veterans could purchase homes using a VA loan for down payment. Originally limited to $2,000 or 50 percent of the total loan, veterans' credit for home mortgages was frequently revised upward to keep up with inflation and changes in the housing market. Business and farm loans were also available through the VA.

By 1961, the annual report of the Veterans Administration recorded a total of 6 million loans (5.6 million for housing under the World War II and Korean War GI Bills). This government generosity stimulated private home ownership. By 1961, over 60 percent of all American families owned their own homes compared to only 44 percent in 1940; GI loans had undoubtedly been a key factor. Of 33 million owner-occupied dwellings in 1961, one out of every six had been financed by VA loans. And, during the 1950s, one out of every five new housing units was purchased with VA help.

A further advantage given to veterans came in preferential hiring in federal and state civil service jobs. This custom of granting "veterans' preference" dated back to the World War I demobilization, but the practice after World War II was more extensive. As a result of joint work by veterans' organizations and the Federal Civil Service Commission, a Veterans' Preference Act was passed in 1944, voted unanimously by the Senate with only one dissenting vote in the House. The act applied to all federal executive branch positions, permanent or temporary. In civil service examinations, veterans would receive five extra points on their scores. Disabled veterans and certain wives, widows, or mothers of disabled or deceased veterans would receive ten points. In addition, the law established a "rule of three." In choosing from a list of three finalists for a position, the selecting official could only pass over a veteran with permission from the Civil Service Commission. In making job cutbacks, veterans were to be retained over non-veterans.

State governments followed suit. California and Kansas awarded ten and fifteen points respectively to state civil service scores of veterans. Others, such as New York and Iowa, gave veterans preference in promotion, and New Jersey exempted decorated veterans from appointment and promotion competitions. Even labor unions promised reinstatement of former members with accumulated seniority for years spent in the armed services. And the Ford Motor Company set up Camp Legion at Dearborn, Michigan, for occupational rehabilitation, medical treatment, and job training for handicapped veterans.

Programs for demobilized GIs more than answered the gravest fears of American policymakers about the possible return of economic depression. The GI Bill poured millions of dollars into training and education, contributed to the promotion of private home ownership, and granted preferential hiring for government positions. By the mid 1960s, expenditures for veterans, including hospital and disablement pay, constituted the fifth largest item of the federal budget. Millions of Americans were touched in some fashion by these programs—as much as half of the population. Veterans' organizations, like the American Legion, the Veterans of Foreign Wars (VFW), Disabled American Veterans, exercised powerful lobbies in Washington. Because, by 1959, more than 50 percent of the federal work force was veterans, a good deal of bureaucratic sympathy for continuing programs operated inside of government. By the end of the 1960s, VA reports demonstrated the effects of such programs. Even for males of equal education, income levels of veterans were significantly higher.

### Male Income by Education Level: 1971

| Education level | Veterans | Nonveterans |
| --- | --- | --- |
| Less than high school | $ 5,700 | $3,740 |
| Some high school | 7,810 | 6,070 |
| High school graduate | 8,740 | 7,470 |
| Some college | 9,610 | 5,940* |
| College graduate | 13,610 | 9,720 |

*Many still attending.
Source: *Administrator of Veterans Affairs*, Annual Report (*1971*), *p. 3.*

☆        ☆        ☆

Despite extensive attention to the problems of veterans and serious thought given to the problem of a possible return to economic depression, the United States did not end the war with a clear vision of social policy. Unity had been achieved, as Kate Smith's phenomenally successful war-bond radio drive revealed in September 1943. Broadcasting for hours without break, Smith begged, threatened, and harmonized her vast radio audience into purchasing bonds. But unity for victory did not mean consensus about the future. Americans still thought very much in terms of the 1930s; haunted by a fear of depression, they still viewed big government as a temporary fixture. Few could even begin to predict the effects of the war on American society. Still children of unemployment and insecurity, Americans in 1945 were largely unaware of the extent to which their lives had been put on a different course by four years of world conflict. As late as 1946, a *Fortune* magazine survey of 1,500 leading businessmen found that a large majority believed a major depression with large-scale unemployment would recur within the next ten years. The face of society had yet to reflect the prosperity and mobility generated by the war. America and Americans looked very much like it and they had in the early 1930s.

Automobiles and railroads still dominated travel inside the United States. The number of civilian aircraft passengers increased rapidly after the war to approximately 12 million per year in 1946 and 1947. But the boom in building aircraft, in increasing average speeds, in upgrading landing and airport facilities, and in transferring freight from ground to air carriers did not occur until the later 1940s and early 1950s.

Patterns of energy consumption during and immediately after the war changed rapidly, although in 1945, the United States remained a coal-dependent society. In 1940, coal provided 52 percent of the nation's energy, with oil, natural gas, and electricity supplying smaller percentages. During and after the war, relative production of coal fell, and consumption from other sources rapidly increased, so that by 1950, oil and natural gas clearly dominated power sources. Coal declined in use in electrical generating, transportation carriers that burned gasoline and oil proliferated, railroads converted to diesel power, and home heating converted to oil and gas. At the same time, per capita expenditure of energy accelerated, primarily because of the boom in automobile use. Still a society dependent upon traditional sources of energy in 1945, the United States in a few years converted to seemingly clean-burning and limitless sources of fossil fuels. Few could anticipate the future price tag of pollution in the nation and political turmoil in the Middle East that this transformation would exact.

In 1945, the United States was still primarily a nation of makers and movers, not of sellers and bureaucrats. It stood on the verge of transformation into a society that consumed goods and information at a rate that would stagger the imagination of the frugal Depression decade. Work in manufacturing, transportation, and mining continued to dominate the economy, but job offerings in these fields increased only marginally after the war. In the case of mining, the number of jobs fell in subsequent decades. The greatest new job opportunities appeared in wholesale and retail work, in state and local government (where employment in twenty-five years more than tripled), in construction, and in finance and insurance.

The geographic distribution of the American population also began a rapid transition in 1945. The Northeast and north central sections of the country still dominated the cultural, economic, and political life of the nation. Large manufacturing cities of the East and Midwest, in turn, dominated these regions. Most of the national political debates centered on traditional battles between urban, ethnic coalitions and disproportionately powerful rural or upstate areas. Although the solid South was the political tail that frequently wagged the Democratic donkey, the financial power associated with New York, Chicago, Cleveland, and other traditional business centers continued to direct the American economy.

Nonetheless, shifts in population, first apparent in the 1920s, became particularly clear after the war. While all regions of the nation experienced growth after 1945, the South and particularly the West greatly increased in population. Population in the West, for example, increased by 40 percent from 1940 to 1950, while the old Northeast gained only about 10 percent. In part, this change resulted from war dislocations—the positioning of military installations and industries in the warmer climates of the South and West made easier by the rapid adoption of home, office, and industrial air conditioning after the war. Perhaps it was also the traditional lure of the West (California always shows up as the place Americans would prefer to live). Possibly it was a combination of all these things. But its one certain effect was the diminished power and importance of the industrial East.

While Americans began to live in new places, they also lived longer. The year 1945 marked the midpoint in a decade of one of the greatest advances in average life expectancy of most Americans. In 1940, the average expectancy for males was about 61 years; for women it was 65. In 1950, this rose to 65.5 years for men and 71 years for women. For black Americans, figures were significantly lower, 51 and 55 in 1940, and 59 and 63 in 1950, although these figures too improved during the period. This increase in longevity touched off important life-cycle changes. For all populations, it meant that large numbers of adults would survive beyond the age of active work into retirement. Although the war intervened to disguise the impact of this increasing longevity, its unexpected effects began to register later in the decade.

One reason for increased longevity was the rapid improvement of medicine during the war. Delivery of medical care and drug discoveries revolutionized the treatment of diseases. By World War II, most, if not all, nutritional diseases were under control. After 1945, for example, pellagra and beriberi were no longer a serious threat to life except in isolated pockets of the country. The properties of certain antibiotics like penicillin had been known to scientists before the war, but medical research and production of such wonder drugs increased rapidly after 1941. In 1942, there was barely enough penicillin manufactured in the United States to treat 100 patients. By late 1943, enough existed to supply all of the Allied armies. During the war, production of streptomycin, first isolated in 1943, also began. By 1945, this drug proved successful in treating cases of tuberculosis and other perennial killers.

Part of this medical success story can be attributed to the entrance of the federal government into research and the diffusion of medical technology. The American armed forces, for example, immunized and treated millions of American men and provided rudimentary instruction in hygiene and the prevention of certain maladies like venereal disease. Federal financing of primary research increased rapidly after the war with reorganization of the National Institutes of Health in 1948 and the National Institute of Mental Health in 1949. Delivery of health care was increasingly shouldered by the federal government after passage of the 1946 Hill-Burton Act, which provided funds for the construction of hospitals—facilities that, unfortunately, remained racially segregated until 1964.

Beyond funding and research, the federal government also extended its record-keeping facilities relating to disease control. The Center for Disease Control in Atlanta, Georgia, took on the task of monitoring the progress and incidence of infectious diseases. Originally called the Communicable Disease Center when it was created in July, 1946, the institution had grown out of a World War II agency specializing in malaria control.

American medicine during and after the war had to treat disabled soldiers. A large number of the patients in VA hospitals after the war were confined for psychiatric disorders—estimates of these run as high as 60 percent. With the need to care for such persons, federal agencies dramatically increased spending for research on problems of mental health. For example, only 2.5 million dollars were spent on research into psychiatry in 1946. By 1947, 27 million were being expended for the same purposes. Facilities for mental patients also rapidly increased; in fact, about 80 percent of all existing psychiatric units in general hospitals were constructed after the war.

Inevitably, during the 1950s and 1960s, American attitudes toward life and death changed under the impact of the medical revolution begun in the war. Wonder drugs, new vaccinations against such diseases as infantile paralysis, and better general health care and delivery systems helped to prolong life. Ironically, however, along with new technologies to cure patients, the waste products of industrial society increasingly took their toll in human-induced diseases such as cancer. Liberated from certain traditional killers, Americans found themselves faced with new diseases in epidemic proportions.

☆ ☆ ☆

While American society in 1945 physically resembled a hard-working, manufacturing and industrial society, whose most serious problems were periodic, capitalist depressions, the war unleashed forces that were incomprehensible to the prewar world. In three domestic areas—technology and communications, the articulation of new social goals, and the aggrandizement of federal institutions—Americans had to face challenges more serious than demobilization or reconversion to consumer production. Undoubtedly, most Americans wanted to return to what they imagined had been the security and good life of the past. This was both impossible, and, a deceptive aspiration. The war laid the foundations for a new stage of social development for which old solutions had little relevance.

Postwar society—even the shape and uses of consumer items—reflected the technological triumphs of World War II production. The civilian application of wartime discoveries often had to await the end of hostilities; nonetheless, new materials and new energy sources and communication systems designed to help defeat the Axis powers revolutionized peacetime production.

The most important new material developed during the war was plastic. Derived from a variety of sources, plastics had long been used for ornamental objects, like combs and billiard balls. New fabrics like nylon first appeared in 1938, and scientists created clear vinyl plastics in the 1930s. However, their wide application as practical substitutes for metal, wood, and rubber was stimulated by wartime shortages of traditional materials and by demands for lighter, but strong and flexible objects. The United States military forces used a wide variety of objects, from synthetic rubber to foamed-plastic bubbles used in submarine buoys to Teflon, Saran, and styrenes. Thus, when Edward Stettinius, Jr., Priorities Director for the Federal Government, and later, Secretary of State, ordered the substitution of plastics for strategic materials in 1941, he was helping to determine the shape of postwar production. By the end of the war, civilian industries were well under way in planning to use plastic substitutes for metals. In 1945, Henry Ford dramatically made this point for the press when he wielded an ax against a plastic experimental car to demonstrate its toughness and resilience.

A new source of energy developed during the war also had wide potential for application. Although its immediate purpose was military, research on a controlled splitting of the uranium atom was kept secret from Vice-President Truman and America's allies, the Russians. Scientists scattered across the United States worked on isolated aspects of harnessing atomic power. Officially called the Manhattan Project and tightly run by Washington bureaucrats, the program successfully achieved a self-sustaining nuclear chain reaction in the laboratory at Stagg Field at the University of Chicago on December 12, 1942. Completion of a workable bomb took two-and-a-half more years; the peacetime application of atomic energy to power generation awaited the 1950s. But the atomic age was born during the war beneath this unused football field.

War also accelerated the invention of new information-retrieval instruments. The war exaggerated the need to compute rapidly, to store and recall information, and to solve complicated mathematical problems. Although work on mechanical calculation began before World War II, several technological breakthroughs occurred after 1939. The binary digit—the basis of computer language—was developed in the 1930s. International Business Machines Corporation (IBM) secured important bookkeeping contracts during the 1930s, including keeping the records of the Social Security Sys-

*The ENIAC computer, developed in 1946. This first large electronic digital computer had 18,000 vacuum tubes and used 140,000 watts of electricity. It used punched cards and plugged wires like those on a telephone switchboard. A quarter-inch computer chip today has far more capacity than the original ENIAC.* (Smithsonian Institution)

tem. During the war, it extended its government operations, working on such defense projects as building a code-breaking machine. By 1944, IBM created its first Automatic Sequence Controlled Calculator, the Mark I, a huge, complicated machine with 500 miles of wires. Only four years later, the company marketed its first commercial electronic computer. The proliferation of information devices and their miniaturization quickly followed, burgeoning into one of the most important postwar industries.

☆              ☆              ☆

By most measures, Americans were unprepared to face the world taking shape during the war in the laboratories and production lines of industry and around the conference tables of the federal government. At best, most people hoped that the terrifying, swerving world of the 1930s would end in a smooth, safe ride into prosperity.

In some respects they were right. Worry about a return to depression was inappropriate after World War II. Despite a flurry of predictions in popular magazines like *Time* and *Life*, the Depression did not recur. Pent-up demand in the form of wartime savings overwhelmed a consumer market shrunken by scarcities. Wage earners, who had saved their salaries because of rationing of consumer goods during the war, bought and ordered goods much faster than they could be produced. For the immediate postwar period, the greatest problems were lagging production and inflation.

Polls taken in 1945 gave no indication of the social and moral convulsions in store for American society. For example, George Gallup estimated that a majority of Americans desired no serious change in the social order once the war ended. Yet, change characterized the new postwar world. A few significant observers saw beyond the status quo when they looked out across American society. They were anything but pleased with the rush to demobilize and reconvert and its attendant emphasis upon restoring traditional values. To the Swedish sociologist and economist Gunnar Myrdal America was approaching an abrupt turning point where the problem of solving racial discrimination could no longer be postponed. This was the hypothesis of his widely discussed work *The American Dilemma*. Undertaken in 1938 with financing by the Carnegie Foundation, Myrdal's study, published in 1944, described a yawning disparity between the promise of American ideals and the experience of black citizens. This, Myrdal wrote, constituted an intolerable burden that must be cast off. Perhaps better than he knew, Myrdal warned that America had developed a defeatist attitude toward social legislation and attempts to improve society through planning and conscious direction. The nation, he wrote in 1944, suffered from "moral overstrain."

Perhaps Myrdal was right about the exhaustion of reform efforts and planning, but this did not mean that Americans were afraid or pessimistic about the future. Writing in 1941 for his publication *Life* magazine, Henry Luce had proclaimed the advent of the "American Century." Viewed from America's shores, the rest of the world lay in ruin. But the world in disarray meant opportunity, not danger, to Luce. Living passionately by its ideals, he advised the United States to feed the world and ply it with the tools of modern technology. The World War remained a world problem, but the solution to world problems belonged to America. There was little need to transform America: We must undertake to be "the Good Samaritan of the entire world."

John Hersey wove the same advice into his bestselling novel of 1944, *A Bell for Adano*. The story focused on Major Victor Jopollo, the American military commander of the small Italian town of Adano. Administering American-style justice in the confused aftermath of Fascism, Joppolo also carefully observed local customs. Although removed by a capricious superior, the commander "represented in miniature what America can and cannot do in Europe." For Hersey, the potential for generosity and optimism hung in the balance. Would America be able to offer the war-weary world the care and good humor of its Major Joppolos?

# 2 A Spoiled Victory

On November 5, Vice-President-elect Harry Truman rushed an enthusiastic telegram to Franklin Delano Roosevelt, his running mate on the Democratic ticket of 1944: "I am very happy over the overwhelming endorsement which you received. Isolationism is dead. Hope to see you soon." Truman was right, if premature. The anxious vigilance of the 1930s was disappearing with every casualty on the beaches of the Pacific Islands, and with every death in European foxholes. It receded a little more at every Allied conference, lost force because of every joint military communiqué and operation, and dimmed after every Voice of America newscast proclaiming America's intention to create a new peaceful world order. Roosevelt had successfully set national policy on a course of internationalism, although it would be several years before this was fully apparent.

As for Truman's veiled request to see the President, nothing much would come of it. F.D.R. brushed off his enthusiastic Vice-President, fully intending to pursue and hold power as he had always done: by sharing it with no one. Truman, like most vice-presidents, dwelt in the obscurity of a functionary's job, anxious to participate but kept in the dark about the secrets of policymaking. And the Missourian was right about who had won the election. It was Roosevelt's victory in the same way that it was Roosevelt's war.

The transition to full-blown internationalism after 1945 was a gradual process involving much more than treaties or declarations of intent. The men who made and articulated American foreign policy in the White House, the State Department, the military, and the Congress first had to be convinced that a broad system of international political agreements could achieve foreign policy aims. The revolution in their thinking during these years amounted to this: a new belief that the United States must pursue its diplomacy in concert with other nations. Perhaps this was the price of predominance, for the exercise of power brought added responsibilities. The internationalism to which Truman alluded coincided with an enormous expenditure of American power everywhere in the world. Before the war, in 1938, the United States had no military alliances, no troops stationed in foreign countries, and a minuscule defense budget. By the end of the 1960s, the United States' military budget approached 80 billion dollars annually. There were over a million-and-a-half military personnel in over 100 countries, and the nation was tied by defense agreements to the destinies of 48 other nations.

The internationalism of World War II emerged from the task of supplying Allied nations and defeating the Axis powers. In the desperate phase of battle, potential American disagreements with the French, English, and especially the Russians faded. The American postwar position, however, gradually became clear. The United States would have both a dependent and an imperial relationship to other nations, dependent in the sense that what happened abroad politically or economically had profound domestic repercussions, and imperial in the sense that the United States became determined to exercise its new power in its own interest.

Postwar internationalism centered on four broad aims. Fundamental was the promotion of the American economic system, through open access to raw materials, secure foreign investments, multilateral trade, and a stable world currency. A corollary of this aim was to support political democracy and economic liberalism where possible. Third was the prevention of the spread of Communism, Socialism, or various forms of economic nationalism that might disrupt the first two goals. A fourth broad aim emerged only gradually, at first as a means of achieving world stability, and then as an end in itself. This was the maintenance of military superiority over the Soviet Union. Of course, foreign policy makers argued over how to achieve these goals. But their general agreement made events that occurred in Berlin, Korea, along the Mekong River in Indochina, or Santiago, Chile, as important as what happened in New York, San Diego, or Kalamazoo, Michigan.

Policies that developed over time did not spring full-blown from the minds of diplomats. Yet, over the years in Washington, distinct patterns of leadership emerged. A remarkable continuity of policy advisers led by Averell Harriman, Clark Clifford, Dean Acheson, John Foster Dulles, Senator Arthur H. Vandenberg, and others developed a coherent view of America's role in world politics. Policy also formed in the crucible of decision-making. Once decided upon, a program of economic and military aid to embattled Greece in 1947, for example, could easily be replicated and expanded in other programs, such as the Marshall Plan for Europe of 1948 or Point Four Aid to underdeveloped countries in 1950.

☆                              ☆                              ☆

During the war, Franklin Roosevelt kept close and jealous control of foreign policy decisions. Wearing three hats—as military commander in chief, as domestic leader, and as head of America's foreign policy apparatus—F.D.R. left a legacy of treaties and agreements as well as a frustrating tradition of ambiguity and postponement. Inactive where he could afford to put off a decision, acutely aware of potential domestic opposition to agreements with the Russians, and determined not to repeat the mistakes of Woodrow Wilson with which he was personally familiar, F.D.R. was more concerned about ending the war than sketching blueprints for a permanent peace. As Dean Acheson, Secretary of State under Harry Truman, later wrote, the President procrastinated in making important foreign policy decisions; he divided administrative power so as to concentrate it in his own hands. He also unrealistically believed in the potential of international universal organizations like the United Nations. From hindsight, Acheson was arguing that, where he had one, Roosevelt's policy exuded optimism. And in a sense, Acheson was right. Wherever Roosevelt did articulate a general policy, in his support for the United Nations or for the Atlantic Charter, he echoed the twenty-five-year-old idealism of Woodrow Wilson's Fourteen Points.

The most important wartime statement setting forth American war aims was drawn up in August 1941, before the United States officially entered the conflict. Partly in fear that the British and Russians, then jointly fighting Hitler, might agree to divide the world into spheres of interest, Roosevelt met with Winston Churchill, the British Prime Minister, at Argenta Harbor, Newfoundland. There, they agreed on an eight-point declaration of principles known as the Atlantic Charter. Beyond a joint commitment to defeat the Nazis, the eight points included support for free trade (except in areas subject to British Empire restrictions), renunciation of war and aggression, and the promotion of world peace, prosperity, and growth. The heart of the document, however, betrayed potential conflicts, and the Russians, when they came to sign it, appended a caveat that certain "historic pecularities of particular countries" would exempt them from following all eight points. The Soviets had points two and three in mind because these rejected "territorial changes that do not accord with the freely expressed wishes of the peoples concerned" and defended "the right of all peoples to choose the form of government under which they will live."

The Russians never really deviated from this position. Time and again they announced they would not tolerate hostile governments in power along their Eastern European borders, no matter how they came to power or what support they enjoyed. More broadly, perhaps, they realized that the two points committed its signatories to a policy that contradicted the aims of revolutionary societies. As aspirations, these two points could only be ambiguous in a world beset by nationalism and economic chaos after the war. Beyond a few countries with a working tradition of parliamentary democracy, modern communications, and economic stability, it is difficult to imagine where the solemn words about self-government used by the framers of the Atlantic Charter might have applied.

In effect, Roosevelt's support for the Atlantic Charter and his public proclamation of the Four Freedoms for the world (freedom of speech, freedom of religion, freedom from want, and freedom from fear) had little specific content. However, in other areas of war strategy, Roosevelt greatly affected the shape of the postwar world. The unconditional surrender of the Axis powers; a United Nations organization to preserve world peace; bipartisanship (meaning Republican agreement) in foreign policy; and a victory in Europe first, with a minimum expenditure of U.S. casualties, were all policies with far-reaching effects. Working with advisers Harry Hopkins, Henry Stimson, Secretary of War General George C. Marshall, and others, Roosevelt often bypassed his Secretary of State Cordell Hull and the State Department bureaucracy. The President preferred personal diplomacy with face-to-face meetings, allowing him to assess the power and intelligence of world leaders, such as Churchill, Stalin, and Chiang Kai-shek of China. This afforded him maneuverability and personal power ordinarily limited by emissaries. But it also meant that the President's policy decisions belonged to him. While he might reap the rewards of success, he would surely also be caught in the whirlwinds of failure.

Several practical decisions flowed from F.D.R.'s support of t conditional surrender proclaimed at the Casablanca Conference with Churchill in January 1943. For example, despite rumors of secret American negotiations in 1945 with German General Wolff for surrender of the Nazi armies in northern Italy, the uncon-ditional surrender pledge preserved the Russian-British-American alliance. When Stalin angrily protested the activities of Allen Dul-les in forwarding German peace feelers to Washington in April, F.D.R. quite rightly replied that the United States and Britain would never consider a separate peace. Also, Roosevelt's decision to build the atomic bomb came partly from his belief that the Allies faced an implacable enemy with whom negotiations were futile. When Roosevelt agreed to American production of a nuclear bomb, he assumed it would be used to put a speedy end to the war. If successful, this awesome weapon would save American lives and bring the Japanese and Geman regimes to their knees.

Roosevelt's attitude toward atomic research demonstrates his style of leadership and hints at what his postwar foreign policy might have been. He was willing to accept limited participation of the British, but even they were acceptable only as junior col-leagues. Despite the urging of scientists such as Niels Bohr, a Danish refugee instrumental in developing atomic theory, F.D.R. refused to share nuclear information with the Soviets or even in-form them of American plans to build a bomb. Roosevelt clearly felt he held a strong hand, and he had no desire to deal away his winning cards.

Roosevelt's commitment to minimizing American casualties also directly affected policy toward the Russians, for it helped shift the burden of defeating the Nazis to the Soviet army. Desperate, as his forces crumbled before the armored divisions of the Germans, Stalin begged Roosevelt and Churchill to open a second European front in order to divert Axis troops from the East. Roosevelt seemed to agree in May 1942, during a Washington conference with Vyacheslav Molotov, the Russian envoy. But lack of prepara-tions, risks, and British losses in their North African colonies di-verted the American effort. The Germans pushed into the indus-trial heartland of the Soviet Union while the United States sped Lend-Lease supplies through submarine-infested waters to Russian ports. But F.D.R. would not agree to a Channel crossing until vast preparations had been completed in 1944. By this time, north Africa (that is, French and British colonies) had been reconquered;

Italy had ceded to the Allies; and the Soviets had hurled back the German Wehrmacht.

When the Soviets reversed the tide of battle at Stalingrad and Leningrad and then began painfully to recapture territory, circumstances changed. Once Russian forces began to push into Poland in early 1944, many of the questions about the shape of Eastern Europe, which engaged diplomats at Teheran in 1943 and later at the Yalta Conference in 1945, became academic. The alliance of convenience cemented by common opposition to Hitler showed signs of disintegration as victory approached.

Roosevelt's reluctance to articulate war aims or to strike a lasting and meaningful bargain with the Russians came in part from his fear of political opposition at home. The President's decision to don the cap of "Dr.-Win-the-War" did not save the Democratic party from a close brush with defeat in the 1942 congressional elections. The new 77th Congress was in no mood to listen to liberal promises about world peace or to vote for domestic reform programs. From this situation, F.D.R. concluded he needed Republican support to achieve approval of United States participation in a United Nations organization. As the President wrote to Stalin in 1945, "You are, I am sure, aware that genuine popular support in the United States is required to carry out any government policy, foreign or domestic."

The unlikely source of crucial bipartisan support came from Senator Arthur Vandenberg, Republican from Michigan. First elected to the Senate in 1928, Vandenberg was a native son of Grand Rapids. He had been a successful editor of the *Grand Rapids Herald* and author of two books on Alexander Hamilton. A determined conservative, he was one of only two senators to oppose recognizing the Soviet Union in 1933. In 1940, he had been, he recalled, "an unsuccessful nonactive, *isolationist* candidate for the presidential nomination." Crediting Pearl Harbor for his conversion to internationalism, he was also reborn as a supporter of bipartisanship in foreign policy during the winter of 1943–1944. Vandenberg's growing importance to F.D.R. and then to Truman placed him in the right spot at the right time to affect policy.

These dual conversions in no way established him as a liberal. They simply made his conservatism more relevant. His prominence among foreign policy supporters gave him power to dampen what enthusiasm existed in the Democratic party to accommodate

Stalin. He firmly opposed "appeasing" Stalin, and he said so vigorously at the United Nations Conference in San Francisco in April 1945, and in the Senate. Whether his attitude stemmed from long-held positions or his desire to please large Polish constituencies in Michigan or his general distaste for the political left, he bitterly opposed Soviet activities in Eastern Europe. The man who wrote in 1946 that the Labour Party victory in England so disgusted him that he would "seriously consider getting out of this miserable business" would never accept Communist revolutions in countries occupied by the Red Army.

Bipartisanship in foreign policy epitomized a political turn in the Roosevelt administration during the early days of the war. The President took a decisive step in deciding to dump Vice-President Wallace in favor of Harry Truman in 1944. Although widely praised for his senatorial investigations into inefficiency in war production, Truman was a relative unknown politically—in other words, he had not impressed fellow senators or the press with his views. Many knew him best as a politico associated with the Missouri Democratic party machine run by boss Thomas Pendergast. Others found him to be a loyal New Deal supporter, but lacking in initiative.

Other representatives of the new administrative order brought to Washington by F.D.R. included Secretary of War Henry L. Stimson; James Forrestal, former president of Dillon, Read and Company; John J. McCloy, member of a New York law firm; and Bernard Baruch, the elder statesman of high finance. While the President kept many of his New Deal advisers—Wallace was designated Secretary of Commerce in 1944, for example—his appointments after 1940 identified his administration with the political center.

Roosevelt edged toward the political center in order to disarm potential critics. Primarily, he hoped to prevent a recurrence of the debacle of 1919 when Woodrow Wilson returned to the United States with a peace treaty unacceptable to Congress. Roosevelt's postwar hopes—like Wilson's—resided in an international peace-keeping organization. A tentative United Nations organization emerged in January 1942, in Washington, when the twenty-six nations fighting the Axis powers declared themselves an alliance devoted to the permanent suppression of aggression. In Moscow, next year, at an October conference of "Four Nations on General Security," China, the U.S.S.R., England, and the United States pledged to create an international organization of sovereign "peace-loving" nations dedicated to the maintenance of international security. By August 1944, plans had progressed sufficiently to hold a conference at Dumbarton Oaks mansion in Washington, D.C., where Britain, the U.S.S.R., the United States, and eventually China agreed upon a general structure (the General Assembly) with equal representation for all nations and a council (the Security Council) with permanent Great Power members and revolving elected members from other countries. In effect, this arrangement acknowledged the predominance of the principal nations of the wartime alliance. Precise details of voting and membership were postponed until the Yalta Conference, where it was agreed that all the great powers could veto nonprocedural actions before the Security Council. General Assembly membership extended to all nations that declared war on the Axis powers by March 1, 1945.

A final conference, held in San Francisco in April 1945, proved to be acrimonious. The Soviet Union demanded Assembly membership for the Ukraine and Byelorussia. Stalin also let it be known that he desired a veto even on procedural matters, a claim which he gave up after talking to Harry Hopkins, who rushed to Moscow to negotiate this point. On the other hand, the United States urged membership for Argentina, a nation that had curried favor with the Axis powers. And, the Americans pressed for the right to preserve regional organizations, such as the inter-American defense system in the Western Hemisphere. When the compromise charter was signed, Argentina, Soviet Byelorussia, and the Ukraine were among its signatories. Article 52, preserving the right to create regional treaties, became the justification for several regional alliances established during the Cold War by the United States and its allies.

Despite American press disapproval of Russian demands, the United States initialed the U.N. Treaty on June 26, 1945. It passed through the United States Senate two days later with almost no dissent. Woodrow Wilson's dream of a covenant of nations devoted to peace was finally achieved, but, by that time, the man most responsible for this victory and a personal link between the two historic efforts to secure it—Franklin Roosevelt—was dead.

Like the Atlantic Charter, the United Nations organization perpetuated the wartime alliance of Great Powers: England, the United States, the U.S.S.R., France, and China. No gathering of equals, the organization reflected a realistic appraisal of world power relationships. Two institutions existed in one: a democratic General Assembly and a Security Council dominated by the Big-Five Alliance. This structure preserved the big power diplomacy of the Allies in postwar international relations.

Other important international institutions to develop from the wartime alliance included the international financial organizations created by the Bretton Woods Agreements of 1944. Secluded for a twenty-two-day conference at Mt. Washington Hotel in Bretton Woods, New Hampshire, delegates from over forty countries discussed serious international financial and economic dislocations. The conference anticipated two principal problems after the war: huge North American balance-of-payments surpluses (the United States in 1944 held about two-thirds of the world's monetary gold stock) and enormous European deficits. Aware that economic depression and inflation following World War I had undermined world political stability in the 1920s and 1930s, Secretary of the Treasury Henry Morgenthau, who presided over the conference, and other American delegates, such as Harry Dexter White, Assistant Secretary of the Treasury, pushed plans to stabilize currency values and international trade. Also conspicuously present was John Maynard Keynes, the distinguished British economist whose theories provided a generation of postwar leaders with fiscal tools to prevent or to control recessions and booms. After World War I, Keynes had published his ominous *Economic Consequences of the Peace* in which he accurately forecast serious economic problems. At Bretton Woods, however, he showed more optimism. He hoped that the International Monetary Fund, for alleviation of balance-of-payments problems between trading nations, and the International Bank for Reconstruction and Development (the World Bank), designed to grant loans to devastated areas, would restore and improve world monetary and trade conditions.

The American delegates encountered reluctance from other allies. First the British and then the Russians made proposals to fit their national needs. Harry Dexter White, of the Treasury Department, developed the American proposals. White's plan aimed to facilitate convertability and to stabilize world currencies with a monetary fund joined by nations who contributed gold and currency to its stocks. In times of serious trade imbalance, members could borrow from this fund. Votes in the governing body would reflect the contribution made by each nation. As White estimated, this would give 25 percent of the vote to the United States and 35 percent to Latin America, so that the Western Hemisphere would have a controlling interest of about 60 percent. The British would control 17 percent and the Russians about 3 percent.

The Russians were reluctant to enter any scheme for international currency stabilization, because Stalin feared interference with Soviet economic autonomy and increased Western influence. Thus, the Russians participated in negotiations and stubbornly wrung concessions from the participants. No doubt Stalin, who wanted to keep Lend-Lease supplies flowing and the Russian-American alliance intact, was delighted by news, which Morgenthau circulated, about the possibility of a $10 billion postwar loan for the U.S.S.R. But, by December 31, 1945, with the war over, Foreign Minister Molotov announced that the Soviets would not participate in the Monetary Fund or the World Bank. Thus, these institutions remained under the control of Western Europe and the United States.

A final aspect of wartime policymaking machinery bequeathed by Roosevelt to his untutored Vice-President was his personal diplomatic style. Like a bright thread, it ran through almost every agreement and policy. Personal diplomacy undoubtedly reflected the President's political acumen, but it was also a policy fraught with confusion. For example, Roosevelt indicated he might agree to a division of the world into spheres of interest, where each major power dominated its designated area, but he refused to commit himself, even though Churchill, fighting for preservation of the British Empire, and Stalin, anxious to assert hegemony over bordering countries, might have preferred such an arrangment.

In the key area of contention and negotiation, then, Roosevelt remained noncommittal. Nonetheless, the problems of Eastern Europe, and particularly of Poland, required solutions. Poland was the terrain on which World War II began and traditionally the corridor of invasion into Russia. For millions of American voters, it was their nostalgic homeland. Roosevelt tried to put off any firm decisions about borders or the composition of a future government. For the Russians, however, settlement of the Polish question formed the bedrock of their policy; they insisted on retaining the boundaries adjusted by the 1939 Russian-German Nonagression Pact, and they demanded a government friendly to the U.S.S.R. Such a settlement would inevitably enrage Polish nationalists, for it changed old boundaries and would suppress political expression of hostility toward the Russians. Aside from strong sentimental ties, the United States had few economic or political interests in that nation. The fate of Poland, however, quickly came to symbolize the fate of all Eastern Europe. As Senator Vandenberg said in a speech on April 2, 1944, Poland was a test case for Soviet cooperation; it was a signal lamp "on these new horizons of our destiny."

In May 1945, Stalin wrote to Churchill his definitive views on Poland: "We insist . . . that only people who have demonstrated by deeds their friendly attitude to the Soviet Union, who are willing . . . to cooperate with the Soviet State, should be consulted on the formation of a future Polish Government." The Soviets never budged from this position. At first, the dispute over Poland centered around who should rule after the war: the refugee government-in-exile in London or the Polish refugees in Moscow. The London Emigrés received Churchill's support, but their relations with the Soviets were cool. In April 1943, when the Germans announced that they had discovered the corpses of thousands of Polish officers buried in Katyn Forest, purportedly murdered by Russian soldiers in 1940, the London Poles denounced the Soviets. The Russians angrily demanded a retraction. When this did not come, they broke all relations with the London government-in-exile, accusing it of fascist collaboration. A month before, however, the Russians had formed the Union of Polish Patriots, around which it began to assemble its own government-in-exile.

At first, neither F.D.R. nor Averell Harriman, the Ambassador to Moscow, reacted strongly to these events. However, in August 1944, as the Red Armies approached the Vistula River near Warsaw, the London Poles, anticipating liberation, called upon their supporters to rise up against the Germans. Suddenly, the Russian drive stalled. Virtually without weapons or supplies, the Warsaw fighters waged a losing battle. Furious and desperate, the London government-in-exile pleaded with Stalin to advance, but he refused, citing a German counteroffensive. When the Russians captured Warsaw, the ranks of Polish supporters loyal to the London government had been decimated.

For American policymakers, these events stood as dramatic proof of Soviet intentions. At one time, more tolerant of Russian aims, Harriman emerged a confirmed cold warrior. George Kennan, recently arrived in the Russian capital, recorded in his memoirs that the uprising was "the most arrogant and unmistakable demonstration of Soviet determination to control Eastern Europe in the post war period." Indeed, by this time, Kennan urged that the United States threaten to cut off Lend-Lease supplies to Russia unless Stalin made major concessions in Poland and other Eastern European countries.

Roosevelt responded to the quickly developing crisis in Eastern Europe by negotiating, compromising, and procrastinating. He postponed action for several reasons, not the least of which was the lack of American power in the region. At the Teheran Conference in 1943 and later at Yalta in February 1945, he sought Stalin's personal assurances of cooperation in Europe. Short of threats to the Soviets, he could do little else, but he also was pursuing his policy of winning the war with as few American casualties as possible, and he wanted Stalin's continued cooperation to end the war against Japan.

In his face-to-face encounters with Stalin and Churchill at Teheran and Yalta, Roosevelt attempted to maintain maneuverability in a rapidly shrinking space. Meeting in late November of 1943 in Iran, Roosevelt tried to convince Stalin to cooperate with American aims and the dictates of the Atlantic Charter. But, he indicated he would not oppose border changes for Poland. Citing his upcoming electoral problems with immigrant American voters, he suggested that Stalin allow the Baltic states of Lithuania, Latvia, and Estonia the right to plebiscite elections before incorporating them into the Soviet Union. In effect, the President seemed to signal that the United States would not fight for self-determination in Eastern Europe.

A year-and-a-half later at Yalta, at the last meeting of Roosevelt with Stalin and Churchill, the Soviets had already recognized their own government in Warsaw, the Lublin regime. Soviet troops occupied much of Eastern Europe and were rushing toward Berlin. American and British troops, after a massive Channel crossing, pushed back the Germans in the West. Roosevelt, however, was still bargaining to get the Russians into the war in Asia, and he and Churchill conceded Stalin's claims to Northern Sakhalin Island and the Kuriles (both north of Japan) as part of the price. Regarding Poland, the Russian leader signed a vague protocol promising free elections and participation by "all democratic and anti-Nazi parties." These ambiguous words left different interpretations open to both sides: thus the legacy of misunderstanding and recrimination. What Stalin thought he had achieved and what the Americans hoped he had promised were two different things. In retrospect, American policymakers often cited the Polish question as the beginning of the Cold War. According to Dean Acheson, Stalin began his "offensive" against the United States in Poland.

On March 30, 1945, Roosevelt, obviously ill and desperately fatigued by his Yalta trip, left for Warm Springs, Georgia, his favorite vacation retreat. Thirteen days later, in the afternoon, Harry Truman entered House Speaker Sam Rayburn's office for a meeting. The Speaker told him to call Presidential Press Secretary Steve Early immediately. Summoned to the White House, Truman undoubtedly suspected he was also being summoned to the Presidency. Roosevelt was dead.

Roosevelt's death in the spring of 1945, when the United States stood one month away from victory in Europe and five months away from V-J Day in the Asian war, created a leadership vacuum. His legacy of half-formulated postwar policy depended on personal understandings with Stalin and Churchill. He left behind nascent institutions: both the Bretton Woods agreements and the United Nations organization had yet to be implemented. The shape of German occupation remained undecided. Issues of loans, war reparations, the extent of Russian influence in Eastern Europe, the nature of governments in formerly hostile countries in the West all required resolution.

In Washington, Roosevelt left an internally divided administration. Secretary of the Treasury Morgenthau, for example, favored the pastoralization or permanent industrial and military dismemberment of Germany. Other cabinet members like Henry Wallace of Commerce favored accommodation with the Russians. Still others proposed a tough policy toward Stalin and the aggressive use of American economic and military might to bend Russian policy. By and large, Roosevelt knew how to balance these opinions: disagreements kept his options open. For Truman, however, policy meant making decisions.

In the spring of 1945, when Truman was sworn in as President, he had little experience in foreign affairs and scant knowledge of negotiations with the Russians or other allies. Perforce, he had to rely on his advisers; he could not afford the luxury of F.D.R.'s intentional ambiguity. Truman felt, on the contrary, that he needed to act quickly and decisively to establish continuity of government and leadership in an inherited administration made up of men of great wealth and influence. Truman initially chose firmness

with the Russians, delighting those in the administration pressing
for a tougher policy. On April 20, Averell Harriman, just returned
from the Soviet Union, met with Truman, Secretary of State Edward Stettinius (Cordell Hull had resigned in late 1944), Under
Secretary of State Joseph C. Grew, and Charles E. Bohlen, the
Department's Russian expert. Harriman advised a firm policy toward Stalin. He warned that the Russians stubbornly believed that
the United States, fearing a depression, would make large concessions to them. The ambassador predicted a "barbarian invasion of
Europe"; as evidence, he cited Russian activities in propping up
the Lublin government in Poland. The United States, he concluded, should demand the letter of agreements signed at Yalta.
Truman assured Harriman that he agreed. The United States
would make "no concession from American principles or traditions
in order to win their favor." Nor would the President shrink from
taking firm control of foreign policy.

Two days later, Soviet Secretary of State Molotov arrived in
Washington, en route to the U.N. convention in San Francisco.
His first meeting with Truman was cordial. But, pressed by Stettinius, Stimson, and Navy Secretary James Forrestal, Truman decided to raise the Polish question. After opening statements the
next day, Truman blamed Russia for disputes over Poland: the
U.S.S.R. had violated the Yalta agreements and had scuttled free
elections. When Molotov tried to explain his country's position,
Truman cut him short. The Russian complained, "I have never
been talked to like that in my life." The President snapped, "Carry
out your agreements and you won't get talked to like that."

Undoubtedly, Truman reached his majority in this exchange; he
demonstrated toughness and quickness, and he signaled the Russians that his administration would be different from its predeces-
sor. But his pugnacious stance, while helping him plug a domestic
leadership vacuum and to raise his stock among a distinguished
and wealthy coterie of anti-Soviet advisers, did damage to the
precarious relations between the United States and the Soviets.
And after initially flexing his diplomatic muscles, Truman himself
began to realize some of the complexity of the issues he first tried
to bluster through.

The closing moments of the war brought a rush of decision-
making and international conferences. To aid him, Truman continued to rely upon Harriman, Forrestal, Stimson, and others, but
he also brought in his own men who were generally not associated

with the New Deal or were even hostile to it. Among these were South Carolina's James F. Byrnes, Dean Acheson, the Attorney General Tom C. Clark, and Kentucky congressman Fred Vinson. Several old New Dealers either jumped the administration ship or, like Henry Wallace, walked the plank of dismissal. This transition was more or less permanent. Truman's appointments in the State Department, especially, remained in office for many years. One member of his generation referred to himself and others as the "old contemptibles."

In dismissing Wallace on September 20, 1946, Truman furnished another sign of his determination to run foreign policy. Many observers also assumed he had declared independence from F.D.R. In late 1945 and 1946, Wallace openly criticized Truman's firm line with the Soviet Union, first at Cabinet meetings and then in public. At issue was the change he detected in American policy since the death of F.D.R.: the United States was on a collision course with the U.S.S.R.

At the conference at Potsdam, Germany, on July 3, 1945, Truman crossed the threshold of deteriorating relations. With Germany prostrate, the Allies had to settle issues of reparations. In the eyes of Truman and Secretary Byrnes, the Russians demanded far too much—$20 billion in reparations from Germany and a shift in Poland's boundaries that would push the western frontier of that nation to the Oder and Western Neisse rivers. The bargain struck at Potsdam was a tenuous compromise, with the question of boundaries unsettled. Occupying forces in each sector of Germany could exact reparations from the territory they occupied, with additional materials promised to Russia in industrial capital from the Anglo-American zones.

Other issues were more or less settled. Stalin agreed to enter the war against Japan, but he remained less cooperative about reversing his policy toward Eastern Europe. Truman's negotiating style was equally tough, influenced in part by the stubborn stance of Stalin and in part by the President's knowledge (received on July 16, 1945) that the United States had successfully exploded a nuclear bomb. These results greatly heartened the Americans, but when Truman briefly alluded to the successful test, Stalin dismissed the news with hopes that the weapon would be used against the Japanese. As everyone realized, however, atomic power was no minor matter. When Truman authorized the use of the bomb against Hiroshima and Nagasaki a few days after the Potsdam Con-

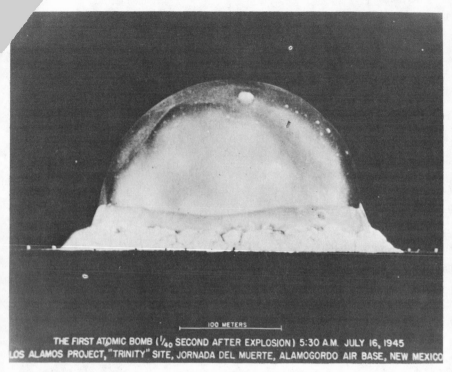

100 METERS

THE FIRST ATOMIC BOMB ($\frac{1}{40}$ SECOND AFTER EXPLOSION) 5:30 A.M. JULY 16, 1945
LOS ALAMOS PROJECT, "TRINITY" SITE, JORNADA DEL MUERTE, ALAMOGORDO AIR BASE, NEW MEXICO

*The first atomic bomb 1/40 second after explosion, 5:30 A.M., July 16, 1945, Los Alamos Project, 'Trinity' Site, Jornada Del Muerte, Alamogordo Air Force Base, New Mexico. (Library of Congress)*

ference, he did so with the intention of terminating the war.
his timing, coinciding with Russia's entry into the Asian war, convinced some observers—among them the Russians—that the
United States intended to exploit the political advantages of its
nuclear monopoly.

Although the President and some members of his entourage,
particularly Secretary of War Stimson, anguished over atomic
energy, Truman probably never seriously considered abandoning
America's monopoly of atomic weaponry, except under circumstances the United States could control. The Baruch Plan, offered
to the United Nations in 1946 by the aging South Carolina mil-
lionaire, proposed to place international nuclear disarmament
under the aegis of the Security Council, with one important pro-
viso: No veto of atomic energy policy would be allowed; until full
control over nuclear weaponry went into effect, the United States
would retain its monopoly. As expected, the Russians rejected the
plan, exercising their Security Council veto. Instead, they
embarked on a crash program to develop their own nuclear
bombs.

Signs of deteriorating relations appeared elsewhere. After initial
flexibility toward governments under its control in Hungary, for
example, the Soviet Union began to tighten its grip in Eastern
Europe. Moreover, in a speech in February 1946, Stalin warned of
the possibility of future capitalist wars, and he announced a new
five-year plan of military and heavy industry expansion. Cited by
many American observers as a declaration of Cold War, the speech
was quickly followed by news of the discovery of a nuclear spy ring
operating in Canada. Many American policymakers were convinced that Stalin had shown his hand.

Two developments on the American side, which occurred
almost simultaneously, indicated a new United States policy. In
reality, however, they only gave intellectual shape and attention to
existing American practice. The first was George Kennan's famous
telegram, solicited by the State Department in February 1946.
This long message proved, beyond the expectations of its author,
to be enormously influential; it was widely circulated in administration circles and published later in *Foreign Affairs* under the
pseudonym Mister X. The other event was public. Winston Churchill, now out of office, responded enthusiastically to Truman's
invitation to deliver an address in Fulton, Missouri, on March 5,
1946. He issued a tough, resounding call to confront the Russians.

Using a phrase he had employed many times before, the Englishman denounced the "Iron Curtain" that had descended across all of Eastern Europe. Truman, sitting on the speaker's dias, and with prior knowledge of the speech's content, seemed to approve his words.

In effect, Kennan's telegram and Churchill's memorable phrases were two variations of the same theme. The first was safer, more hesitant and accommodating; the second was harsh and bellicose. But they marked the parameters of American foreign policy thinking and indicated the relatively narrow kind of assumptions that guided American strategies of containment in the Cold War.

Composed in haste, the Mister X telegram summarized Kennan's experience since 1944 in the Soviet Union. In sections, "all neatly divided, like an eighteenth century Protestant sermon," he recalled that he had wanted to convince the leaders of the United States to oppose Russian feints and maneuvers, to block infiltrations and shore up weak spots: in effect, to contain expansion. This last idea meant, in his words, to maintain, "a long-term, patient but firm and vigilant containment of Russian expansive tendencies." This American counterforce would mellow aggressive tendencies in the U.S.S.R. Somewhat later, Kennan claimed that policymakers distorted his meaning by emphasizing only military containment, but some of the blame must be his. The essay bristled with expressions like "fanaticism" and "the innate antagonism between capitalism and socialism" and presented an extraordinary picture of Communists all over the world, drawn from the old RCA advertisement: "Like the white dog before the phonograph, they hear only the 'master's voice.'" Stripped of its subtleties, Kennan's essay probably said what many policymakers had already decided: Russian and Communist penetration into any new area in the world must be stopped. Furthermore, it assumed that all Communists, whatever their nationality, only obeyed their master's voice from the Kremlin. Finally, the essay offered the hope of future resolution in the struggle: the Soviets would finally relent.

Churchill's speech at Fulton, on the other hand, was simple and militant. The deposed British Prime Minister demanded an English-American alliance to defend "Christian civilization." Equating Fascism and Communism, he stressed military opposition to Russian policy. It would be a dangerous and awe-inspiring moment, he believed, but "the United States stands at this time at the pinnacle of world power." He hoped that power would join in service to his crusade.

## Cold War Europe, 1950

ICELAND

GREAT BRITAIN

NORTH SEA

IRELAND

ATLANTIC OCEAN

NORWAY

SWEDEN

FINLAND

BALTIC SEA

DENMARK

U.S. Zone

THE NETHERLANDS

GERMAN DEM. REP.

Berlin

British Zone

FED. GERMAN REP.

Soviet Zone

4-POWER OCCUPATION

POLAND

U.S.S.R.

BELGIUM

LUX.

French Zone

U.S. Zone

FRANCE

SWITZ.

AUSTRIA

CZECHOSLOVAKIA

HUNGARY

RUMANIA

PORTUGAL

SPAIN

ITALY

YUGOSLAVIA

BULGARIA

BLACK SEA

ALBANIA

TURKEY
(Joined NATO 1951)

GREECE
(Joined NATO 1951)

SPANISH MOROCCO

MEDITERRANEAN SEA

MALTA
(Br.)

MOROCCO

ALGERIA

TUNISIA

| | NATO nations | | Communist nations |
|---|---|---|---|
| | Neutral nations | 0 | 500 |

Miles

The Iron Curtain speech had a remarkable success in defining the purposes of American foreign policy. Kennan's essay, published in July 1947, also drew widespread praise. But there were still dissenters who felt that even the Mister X article was far too harsh. Most notable among these was political columnist Walter Lippmann. In several essays, Lippmann sharply rebuked Kennan for his lack of realism. Containment as proposed and practiced, he wrote, was "fundamentally unsound," yet he feared this represented the best of State Department thinking. Remarkably prescient, he stated that containment would require too much planning and bureaucracy and would incur huge military expenditures that would revolutionize American society. Moreover, the policy seemed conservative and negative. Instead of pursuing peace first, it would assert power, and in areas where the United States could least afford to extend itself. Finally, he wrote, it was folly for the United States to try to make "Jeffersonian democrats out of the peasants of eastern Europe, the tribal chieftains, the feudal lords, the pashas, and the warlords of the Middle East and Asia."

Right in so many of his criticisms, Lippmann also understood that the Truman administration had chosen containment, not accommodation, by 1946. Occasionally, the administration doubted the wisdom of this choice, but the general direction had been set. Roosevelt's wartime internationalism evolved from a tenuous partnership of great powers into a policy that was perhaps implicit all the while: a redefinition of the world into spheres of interest. This is precisely what most policymakers had strenuously opposed, but it is what containment inevitably meant. Because containment implied limiting Soviet influence to its contiguous areas, the American sphere of interest remained huge and amorphous, encompassing Western Europe, Latin America, and many of the former Asian and African colonies of Britain and France. Unfortunately, this extended strategy defined every revolt, or nationalist revolution, and every attack on private property as a threat to American policy.

☆             ☆             ☆

World War II ended with one of the most decisive military victories in modern history. Yet, for all the good will generated in the heroic struggle against the Axis, the alliance between the Americans and the Russians degenerated into a squabble over the spoils. Good relations corroded rapidly into suspicions and antagonistic opposition. Perhaps this icy bath might never have been drawn, but only the magnanimity, understanding, and generosity possessed by few men could have altered the course of Cold War events. A different United States policy would have meant treating the Soviet Union more as a partner and less as a conquered nation. It would have demanded a degree of political sophistication probably undeveloped at the time. And, it would have demanded a degree of cooperation and understanding from the Soviet side that is very difficult to imagine. Had F.D.R. lived longer into the postwar period, American policy might have remained more flexible. But in reality, both sides came to feel that a hard line expressed their national interest.

As developed in acts and policy statements, the Cold War policy of the United States after Truman varied from time to time and place to place. Presidents Eisenhower, Kennedy, and Johnson, who followed its basic tenets, varied their approaches. Whole areas of the world escaped the Cold War and competition between superpowers. In Western Europe, American Cold War policy encouraged a remarkable reconstruction. Frequently, however, American policy was rigid and supportive of petty tyrants and dictators, such as Batista in Cuba, Duvalier in Haiti, the Shah of Iran, and Ngo Dinh Diem of South Vietnam. Over the years, the policy seemed to lose the subtleties and purposes enunciated by Kennan, until two overweening assumptions remained: support for American business interests and opposition to Communism.

Ironically, the division of the world was precisely what containment hoped to prevent; the United States itself promoted the polarization of the world into Communist and capitalist parties. Despite rumblings in Congress and bellicose campaign promises, the United States could not prevent the spread of Communism. Peace eluded Truman and those fellow practitioners of Cold War policies who followed him. The United States in 1950 found itself mired in a Korean War it could not win, and in the 1960s, in a struggle in Vietnam it had neither the heart nor the energy to conclude. The prosperity and economic stability sought by containing Russian influence was a glittering prize brought home in the 1950s and 1960s. But gilt-edged American economic success could not disguise the fact that, by the measure of its own goals, Cold War policy did not prevent the division of the world into two hostile camps.

# 3 Family Culture

In the last scene of the epochal film *Giant* (1956), an elderly Texas couple, played by Elizabeth Taylor and Rock Hudson, relax for the first time in 201 minutes. Recalling their good life together, they look approvingly at the baby crib at the end of the room. Here, two grandchildren, one obviously Anglo-Saxon, the other Mexican, smile into the camera. And, behind them, through the open window, the camera brings into focus another symbol of integration, a white sheep and a black Angus calf standing side by side. Thus, George Stevens's remarkably successful film ends in a vision of marriage and the perpetuation of the family as the solution to immense social problems.

This family ideology figured in a thousand ways in Hollywood movies in the 1940s and 1950s. Countless films ended in the same fashion, as if to say that romance, marriage, and children were sufficient goals for Americans: if only Americans strengthened the bonds of kinship, then the frightening transformations of modern life could be comprehended. Thus, in *Giant*, the struggle over racial integration becomes an episode in the renewal of family ties. In that film, East merges with West, civilization is united to the frontier, and two races join in marriage in a visual hymn to the American family.

During the same years, however, Hollywood made as many films that focused on the unraveling of the American family structure, in which divorce, extramarital love, alcoholism, and juvenile delinquency shattered the ideal of bliss and turned American men, women, and children into hostile, warring generations. James Dean, who played a grown-up delinquent in *Giant*, had only one year earlier achieved his first acting triumph in *East of Eden*. In that movie, the message was simple, but reversed: The American family was deeply troubled; parents lacked understanding. The result was tormented youth and generational conflict.

Americans have long lived with contradictory attitudes about the success of the family as a social institution. This immense subject has been a staple of modern culture in novels, films, and popular psychology and sociology. Yet the period after World War II owes some of its special character to unique developments in the social and cultural history of the family.

From the 1940s to the 1960s, Americans looked at the family with double vision: with optimism and despair. In one of the most popular novels of the period, J. D. Salinger's *Catcher in the Rye*, published in 1951, both visions exist. The contradictory attitudes of his society toward the family confuse the adolescent hero, Holden Caulfield. In his search for authenticity, he discovers only "phoniness"; instead of fathers, he finds betrayers. Yet Salinger's much-censored book ends affirmatively. After scrambling down the rungs of his private hell, Holden returns home with a larger, more tolerant view of society. He decides to live with contradiction.

A sense of the importance of—and a tone of worry about—the family and of the changing roles of parents and children was pervasive, even tingeing child-rearing and baby-care books. The remarkable sales of Dr. Benjamin Spock's *Baby and Child Care* book reveal a deep popular concern for family health in the decades following 1945. Between 1946, when it was published, and 1976, the pocket edition of this work sold over 23 million copies. Only the Bible and the combined works of Mickey Spillane and of Dr. Seuss sold significantly more copies. Spock's work was not entirely new, for it built upon previous child-rearing advice books, but the author was one of the first to popularize the theories of Sigmund Freud and of the American philosopher John Dewey. From these thinkers, Spock drew a theory of child-rearing designed to create well-adjusted individuals—a generation of guiltless, happy adults who could move easily into a modern world of large, socialized institutions. As he put it: "How happily a person gets along as an adult in his job, in his family and social life, depends a great deal on how he got along with other children when he was young." Early behavior depended upon mothers and fathers. In most cases, Spock advised, parents should follow their instincts with their children: "Trust your own instincts, and follow the directions that your doctor gives you." In many cases, a child could indicate what was best for him. As for parenting roles, the bulk of the obligation should fall to the mother, although a father might change diapers or make formula on Sundays.

It is difficult to measure the influence of Spock's advice on the parents who read the baby book. Many, if not most, probably got no further in the index than "measles symptoms" or "diaper rash." Yet Spock fully intended to help liberate the modern family from the long, repressive reach of tradition. Publication of his book signaled the important ideal of a child-centered, family-centered America on the verge of unprecedented prosperity and optimism.

Although the most popular, Benjamin Spock was not the only child-rearing expert in this era. The psychologist B. F. Skinner offered a remarkably different notion of the American family and of child-rearing for those who carefully read his utopian novel *Walden Two* (1948). In his books following World War II, Skinner proved himself to be one of the most inventive and controversial of modern behaviorist psychologists. In this period, he developed two significant inventions: the teaching machine and the "air crib." These instruments, intended to replace or aid teachers and parents, suggest the implicit direction of his thinking about child-rearing. The hopes of rationality and traditional religion had been dashed in Fascism, depression, and world war. Skinner proposed to raise a new generation of Americans, unaffected by guilt or misguided by false beliefs in religion and reason, which had been wrongly instilled by indulgent parents.

*Walden Two*, named after Henry David Thoreau's famous nineteenth-century book, described a perfected society incorporating management practices, equality, elimination of the family, and behavioral conditioning of children. Skinner suggested that the community, not the biological parents, assume the risks and rewards of child-rearing. He implied that excessive parental love was a key to the failure of Americans to adjust to modern society.

Both Spock and Skinner, in their own ways, responded to strong forces reshaping the American family. Some of these encouraged the view that family stability was increasing. Other trends appeared to threaten the very existence of the institution. As the economy changed, as more women sought full-time employment, as trends in marriage, birth, and divorce rates and in family size shifted rapidly, the shape of the family seemed to be evolving in several directions at once. No wonder, then, that American culture reflected contradictory attitudes toward this institution.

✩               ✩               ✩

After the war, the American family experienced the inconveniences and stresses of reconversion to peacetime living. Millions of women with absent husbands and children with absent fathers suddenly confronted returning GIs. Readjustment often proved difficult for both men and women. Demobilized soldiers had jobs or careers to resume or possibly several years of school under the generous provisions of the GI Bill. In industry, returning GIs resumed seniority in unions and took up jobs on the production line or in offices. This was not always an easy readjustment, as William Wyler's sympathetic film *The Best Years of Our Lives* depicted in 1946. Yet the problems faced by women were probably as disruptive. Returning soldiers and closed munitions plants spelled fewer jobs for women. While many of these workers intended to stay on the job, millions were forced out of the factory and into the home.

An enormous surge in divorce rates in 1946 suggests that these problems sometimes became too serious to settle. The year 1946 was an extraordinary year: 18.2 percent of existing marriages were dissolved, a rate significantly higher than the years on either side of this date. Although the divorce rate rose during the war to around 14 percent, 1946 represented the peak year, for the rate gradually dropped back to about 10 percent in 1950, where it remained stable for several years. As the two tables following show, the divorce rate rose sharply after the war, declined to a plane fifteen years in length, and then rose abruptly after 1968. Only post-1973 divorce rates equaled the high percentage that prevailed briefly in 1945 and 1946.

The impact of the war on family life also registered in marriage rates. Most countries fighting in World War II experienced significant increases in marriage rates, but the United States showed a particularly striking percentage of persons over fifteen who married. From 1944 to 1948, the United States had the highest mar-

*Divorce as a Percentage of Existing Marriages*

| 1942 | 10.0% | 1947 | 13.9% |
|------|-------|------|-------|
| 1943 | 10.9  | 1948 | 11.6  |
| 1944 | 12.3  | 1949 | 10.6  |
| 1945 | 14.3  | 1950 | 10.2  |
| 1946 | 18.2  | 1951 | 9.9   |

Source: *Paul Jacobson*, American Marriage and Divorce (*New York: Rinehart, 1959*), p. 90.

*Divorce as a Percentage of 1,000 Population*
*(by 2-year intervals)*

| 1944 | 2.9% | 1958 | 2.1% |
|---|---|---|---|
| 1946 | 4.3 | 1960 | 2.2 |
| 1948 | 2.8 | 1962 | 2.2 |
| 1950 | 2.6 | 1964 | 2.4 |
| 1952 | 2.5 | 1966 | 2.5 |
| 1954 | 2.4 | 1968 | 2.9 |
| 1956 | 2.3 | 1970 | 3.5 |

Source: Historical Statistics of the United States, *Bicentennial Edition,*
*Vol. I, p. 64.*

riage rate of any reporting country in the world, except Egypt. This statistic means that a higher percentage of Americans married than before or since that interval. Almost 70 percent of males and 67 percent of females over fifteen were married in 1950. Compared to figures collected during the Depression, this statistic represents a large increase. In 1946, the number of eligible persons who married during that year was almost twice the proportion joined in wedlock during 1932.

The consequence of the marriage boom and of lower average marriage ages was a baby boom: more marriages meant more children. The number of live births also increased because of other factors. The illegitimacy rate rose much faster than in previous periods, although this increase occurred in tandem with the higher rates for legitimate births from 1940 to 1957. The infant mortality rate (fetal death ratio) dropped significantly after World War II, reflecting major advances in obstetrics and also a rapid increase in the percentage of births in hospitals.

The American desire for larger families also pushed the baby boom. Translated into statistics, this desire of parents for more children showed up in an exceptional upward curve in the generally downward trend toward fewer children and smaller families typical of most of the twentieth century. Birth-rate figures illustrate this trend.

The war-induced postponements of marriage and children partly account for the precipitate rise in family formation and births.

#### Percentage of Hospital Births by Year and Race

| White | | Nonwhite | |
| --- | --- | --- | --- |
| Year | Percentage | Year | Percentage |
| 1940 | 59.9% | 1940 | 27.0% |
| 1950 | 84.3 | 1950 | 57.9 |
| 1967 | 99.4 | 1967 | 92.9 |

Source: *National Center for Health Statistics*, Natality Statistics
Analysis, U.S., 1965–1967, *p. 20.*

Another factor was the undoubted prosperity that many Americans
experienced. (The gross national product doubled between 1945
and 1962.) Because of the postwar employment boom and few new
immigrants, many Americans increased the size of their families in
anticipation of continued economic stability. Although unmeasur-
able, the widespread emphasis upon family values, plus federal
economic stimulation in areas like home ownership, undoubtedly
registered in these statistics. After the Depression, the years following the war seemed to fulfill a middle-class dream of prosperity
and security.

More intensely involved than ever before in marital arrange-

#### *Birth Rate: Birth Rate per 1,000 population*
*(by 2-year intervals)*

| Date | Percentage | Date | Percentage |
| --- | --- | --- | --- |
| 1940 | 19.4% | 1956 | 25.2% |
| 1942 | 22.2 | 1958 | 24.5 |
| 1944 | 21.2 | 1960 | 24.0 |
| 1946 | 24.1 | 1962 | 23.3 |
| 1948 | 24.9 | 1964 | 21.7 |
| 1950 | 24.1 | 1966 | 19.4 |
| 1952 | 25.1 | 1968 | 17.4 |
| 1954 | 25.3 | | |

Source: *National Center for Health Statistics*, Natality Statistics
Analysis, U.S., 1965–1967, *p. 2.*

An American view of women in the 1950s: "American women are struggling to fill new functions and responsibilities, to work out a new way of life in response to changing conditions: the daylong absence of the modern husband from the home; the lack of household servants; the public expectation that women will act as members of their communities and the world, as well as of their families; and the idealistic American conception of the wife's role that only the rare woman could fulfill. With the feminists' battle long behind them, U.S. women are less interested in being poets and statesmen then they were 25 years ago, and more interested in domesticity."

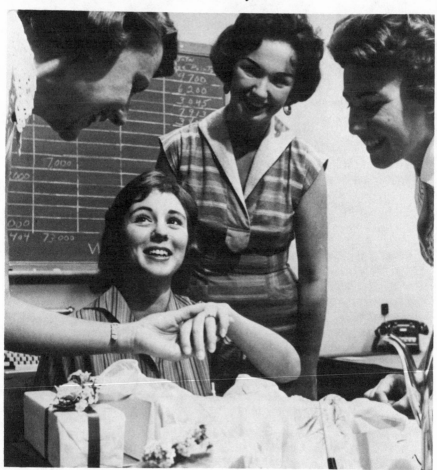

"Thirty-five percent of U.S. women hold daily jobs outside the home. The working woman may be an executive, but, eighteen times oftener, is a subordinate. And many a girl's happiest day at the office is the day she leaves to get married."     (National Archives)

*"The Glorified American Girl is a prime element in U.S. mythology, but American men continue to marry 'the girl next door,' who bears only a family resemblance to the love goddess."*    (National Archives)

ments, Americans also talked, thought, and debated about the stability and future of this institution, sometimes as if the future of society and victory in the Cold War depended upon it. New institutions to deal with family problems, developed by psychologists, indicated widespread concern for the continued health of the family.

Although the profession of marriage counseling appeared in the 1930s, it expanded enormously after the war in concert with a general increased interest in psychology. Up to the Depression, the mental health movement concerned itself primarily with individual adjustment and therapy. After the war, interest began to shift to the context of the family. In the 1950s, this attention became an organized movement. Beginning in 1950, with the formation of the Committee on the Family as part of the Group for the Advancement of Psychiatry headed by the noted psychologist William C. Menninger, the practice of family therapists spread in psychological circles. By 1956, this approach had become respectable and established.

Public opinion also reflected keen interest in the health of the family unit. Just after the war, the Gallup poll published a survey indicating that about 35 percent of Americans desired stricter divorce laws, 31 percent felt they should be unchanged, and only 9 percent thought they should be relaxed. Although some differences of opinion reflected age groups, with older people supporting a stricter marriage code, other surveys uncovered majoritarian conservative attitudes that disapproved of women wearing slacks or shorts in public or occupying public office.

Conservative attitudes toward the family, particularly enunciated by the Catholic Church, made legislators and health officials reluctant to legalize or disseminate information about birth-control devices. For the first two decades following the war, federal and state laws generally prohibited easy access to methods of family planning and limitation. This prohibition did not prevent widespread recourse to contraceptives and illegal abortions, but it did express and uphold an older, religiously sanctioned view of the family.

Nonetheless, during the 1950s, rapid progress marked the technology of birth control: the intrauterine device was reinvented, and researchers developed oral contraceptives from women. Although opposed by the official hierarchy of the Catholic Church, contraception by birth-control devices was promoted by Protestants. In 1961, for example, the National Council of Churches reported favorably on family planning schemes. Those states, such as Connecticut and New York, with legislative bans on the sale of contraceptives gradually eased their restrictions. The result was a franker and more open discussion of birth control and sexuality, increased activities by planned parenthood associations, and the legal use of contraceptives. By the middle 1960s, a number of population experts could realistically envision a drastic cut in the birth rate to effect zero growth in population.

As a method of birth control, abortion remained illegal throughout the United States until well into the 1960s. The problem of widespread illegal abortions, however, received widespread attention as early as 1955 at a conference on abortion sponsored by the Planned Parenthood Federation of America. Four years later, the American Law Institute, in its Model Penal Code, proposed revision of state bans on abortions for reasons of health, for risk of deformity, or for conception resulting from rape or incest. Although some states, such as Maryland, enacted such legislation, not until January 1973, when the United States Supreme Court in *Roe* v. *Wade* and *Doe* v. *Bolton* struck down the abortion laws on the grounds of invasion of privacy, did therapeutic termination become universally legal.

With so much attention given to child-rearing, the role of women in marriage attracted a great deal of discussion. Many American women held jobs after the war—over 2 million more in 1946 than in 1940—but others were forced out of work or voluntarily returned to the family. They were encouraged to do so by a popular culture that pictured domesticity as the most rewarding goal in life. From the nostalgic view of child-rearing in the bestselling family biography *Cheaper by the Dozen* to the pages of ladies' magazines, the message remained the same: house and garden were the ideal environment for American women. A good example of this ideology appeared in *McCall's Complete Book of Bazaars*, an advice book for holding a successful charity gathering. Obviously aimed at the middle-class suburban housewife, the book promised that a successful bazaar would create a feeling of "identification" in the community, as well as uncover hidden talent of neighbors. "A bazaar," the tract solemnly proclaimed, "can be a miniature world of its own, for the potentialities and challenges it offers are manifold."

The middle-class ideal for the family required prosperous suburban living. Success rested upon the ingenuity of the wife, who had to master different and conflicting roles. As mother, she guided the socialization of her children; as family manager, she directed the consumption of new household products; as sexual partner and seductress, she cemented the loyalty and attention of her husband. While certainly a stereotype, this view of women's roles existed in countless popular women's magazines that filled their pages with cooking tips, household cleaning advice, and short, romantic stories stressing the rewards of female sacrifice. Dubbed "the feminine mystique" by writer Betty Friedan in 1963, this ideology operated as a powerful justification for believing that the family was the most important institution in society. Because being a housewife was the most rewarding career, those women who worked or remained single risked guilt and neurosis.

Friedan's negative description of the miniature world of suburban housewifery probably exaggerated the pervasiveness and the uniqueness of the feminine mystique, but it did accurately reflect the picture of women in popular culture. While the idealized family was obviously a middle-class institution, even those few explicit portrayals of the working class, such as Jackie Gleason's *The Honeymooners*, expressed variations on the same theme. The majority of television programs indulged America's love affair with family life. By the mid-1950s, television had replaced the movies as the basic medium of family entertainment. As film companies in desperation began to aim their product toward specialized audiences, such as teenagers, television captured the family and adopted a conservative model of the institution.

Early television's most perfect family was the Andersons of *Father Knows Best*, a series that ran for eight years after 1954 on CBS and NBC and then survived in reruns on ABC. Although exhibiting a timeless quality, *Father Knows Best* mirrored postwar America. As if to signal the end of the Depression and the war era and the beginning of a hopeful and secure age, the producers of the show chose a title song, "Just Around the Corner There's a Rainbow in the Sky."

Initially a radio program begun in 1949, the series explored the troubles and triumphs of an American middle-class family, presided over by a wise and kindly father played by Robert Young. The town and characters were as typical and idealized as a Norman Rockwell cover for the *Saturday Evening Post*: Maple Street, Springfield, was an address with countless resonances in the col-

In this publicity still from Father Knows Best, *the mirror image of actor Robert Young serves to emphasize the importance of the character he played.* (NYPL Picture Collection)

lective memory and literary imagination. As manager of the General Insurance Company, Jim Anderson exercised his patient and benign rule over his wife, Margaret, and three children. So seriously did Robert Young take this role as paternal protector of the American family, that he sometimes stepped across the fictional frontier into real life. Thus, in 1950, he began an extensive campaign for safe driving, using his show to convince teenagers to modify their driving habits.

A comic variation on the ideal family and television's most popular production of the 1950s was the *I Love Lucy Show*. From its beginning in 1951, the show enjoyed an enormous success. The setting was apartment life in New York City; the two main characters were Lucy and her Cuban-born (and real-life) husband, Ricky Ricardo. Although the couple had no children initially, an upstairs couple, Fred and Ethel Mertz, acted sometimes as friends, sometimes as grandparents. When Lucille Ball became pregnant, the pregnancy and birth were written into the show. On Monday, January 19, 1953, one of the largest television audiences ever assembled heard the announcement of the birth of a son.

The premises of the show were comic, and the situations Lucy found herself in varied considerably, but each episode renewed the battle of the sexes. Ricardo was a popular bandleader. And whatever she did, Lucy could never achieve her greatest goal: to be an actor, a singer, a dancer, a star equal to her husband. Her aspirations always ended in chaos and comic hopelessness. The "situation" always resolved itself, however, as she resigned herself to being a housewife and helpmate.

The show ended in real-life divorce in 1960 (since 1957, the series had been replaced by hourly specials). In 1962, however, Lucille Ball returned with Vivian Vance on the *Lucy Show* in a situation without husbands. Their new series also proved to be enormously popular, and its success suggested that the television comedy format could do far more than reflect the traditional boundaries of home life. Its success indicated that the paternal, nuclear family was not the only living arrangement acceptable to Americans. The reality of American family life had become far broader, looser, and diverse than an ideal mother, father, and children living in pleasant harmony. Americans were well aware of this fact in the early 1960s. By the end of the 1960s, the broken family appeared as a staple in popular culture.

☆              ☆              ☆

Contrary to the hopes of a great many Americans after the war, the family sustained changes that threatened to alter its traditional form. These changes appeared in two varieties: some threatened the traditional nuclear family, while others fundamentally altered relationships within the institution. Divorce, long the most ominous threat to the family, began to increase after 1958, rising rapidly in the late 1960s and 1970s. Pressure on relationships inside the family mounted with the steady increase in the number and percentage of married working women. By the end of the 1960s, the American family began to assume the characteristics of a dual nuclear family, with two centers: a husband and wife sharing both the task of breadwinner and the prerogatives of the role.

Although one part of the statistical profile of the family revealed stability and continuity in the period after 1945, a number of disruptive trends also emerged shortly after 1945. Early marriages and births out of wedlock increased rapidly. In 1940, the median age at the time of a first marriage for men was 24.3 years; for women, it was 21.5. By 1968, this figure fell to 23.1 and 20.8 years respectively. In real terms, this meant many marriages with one or both partners still in the teenage years.

The rapid rise in illegitimacy rates—quadrupling between 1940 and 1970—enormously increased the number of single-parent family arrangements, most of them headed by women. While the number of households headed by women by no means approached the number headed by men, their growth was approximately twice the rate of two-parent families after 1940. These changes were especially striking in the black population. By 1974, about 29 percent of all households headed by women were black, even though the percentage of black households in the population was only about 11. Such disproportionate figures gave rise to a sociology of broken families and cultural deprivation affirming that single-parent families breed delinquency and criminality. As the 1955 report of the Congressional Joint Committee on the Economic Report said: "Broken families are more common in the low-income group. One seventh of the low-income urban families included one adult and one or more children but only one-twentieth of the middle income families were of similar structure." To some sociologists, this set of facts explained higher incidences of crime, unemployment, and other social ills among poorer populations.

If the feminine mystique aimed at creating competent, happy

women devoted to child-rearing, then rising juvenile delinquency figures, especially in the suburbs, suggested their failure. After 1948, official juvenile court case records and FBI arrest tallies for children under eighteen years old recorded a sharp increase in apprehensions and trials of young people. Almost every year, police arrested more children for crimes ranging from breaking curfews and smashing windows to criminal theft and murder. Crime rates for adults increased as rapidly, but teenage delinquency particularly worried social workers, sociologists, criminologists, and psychologists, all of whom agreed that the broken family breeds delinquency. For all the beneficial influences of suburban living—the idealized family, "togetherness," and permissive upbringing—children appeared to suffer acute alienation from their parents that they expressed in antisocial acts. And, as the average age of the American population plunged in the late 1950s and early 1960s, this trend threatened to persist.

Working women changed the family most significantly in this period. Over a ninety-year period, the percentage of women working rose from about 19 in 1890 to 43 in 1970. Most of this increase came from the entry of married women into the labor market. This group rose from a mere 5 percent in 1890 to around 41 percent in 1970. Significantly, one of the largest increases in women's employment occurred during the 1950s, a fact that may help explain the prosperity felt by many American families. (Increased employment did not necessarily mean increased career opportunity. This fact can be illustrated by changing percentages of women receiving master's and doctoral degrees. In the mid-1930s, women received 13 percent of Ph.D. and 37 percent of M.A. degrees. By the mid-1950s, this portion had shrunk to 9 percent of Ph.D. and only 33 percent of M.A. degrees.) The effects of this change in women's employment, of course, were experienced differently by different classes and in different regions of the United States. Nonetheless, rising employment provided a major key in the development of a strong women's movement in the 1960s.

A final large demographic shift that altered the basis of the traditional nuclear family was increased longevity. The average age expectancy increased by about five years between 1945 and 1970. This was a change of some significance. It meant that many more people could hope to live several years beyond retirement. Looked at comparatively, it also meant that women outlived men by an average of seven years in 1970 as opposed to four years in 1945. Another comparison indicates that blacks increased their longevity by a much higher percentage than whites, so that by 1970, this segment of the population lived, on the average, to sixty-five years.

Altogether, these figures point to an increasing part of the population that was either childless or characterized by the absence of one spouse through death or divorce. This extended period of later life, referred to by the French as the "third age," became increasingly important after the war, although its effects were temporarily masked by the marriage boom and baby boom. Despite the focus on youth in the 1950s and 1960s, the American population grew steadily older. The percentage of married persons living beyond sixty-five years of age increased after 1940, and the absolute numbers of single, elderly people increased. Among elderly Americans, widowed women constituted by far the largest group, with almost 30 percent surviving beyond sixty-five.

Political power of aged Americans first emerged during the 1930s in the Townsendites, a grass-roots movement that promised to end poverty among the retired. The passage of the Social Security Act in 1935 and its subsequent modifications, however, established policy for dealing with America's elderly. Primarily a strategy to convince workers to retire by providing income security, the program succeeded, but not without controversy. Millions of workers retired with some steady income; at the same time, inadequate funds for medical care, unemployment, boredom, and alienation plagued older Americans. The Golden Age movement, beginning in 1940, tried to confront these problems, as did the *Senior Citizen*, a journal first published in January 1955. Despite these efforts, the addition of large numbers of citizens in the third age, created a group whose primary interests were neither marriage nor children. Many of them felt out of place in a family-oriented society, living a precarious existence in the retirement or nursing homes that spread rapidly after the war.

Modifications in laws concerning the status of families reflected the changing structure of American family life. Sociologists and anthropologists called the resulting legal institution a "companionship family," or sometimes, a "democratic family." In essence, this language implied increased freedom—sanctioned by law—ensuring individuals more latitude in choosing a marriage partner or in deciding to break off a relationship. Where the community and parents once severely curbed individual freedom, the state established liberal guidelines for divorce, inheritance, legitimacy, and the selection of marriage partners. At the same time, society more readily invaded family privacy. For example, in 1971, the United States Supreme Court, in *Wyman* v. *James*, ruled that social workers could enter the home in the interests of a child member, against the wishes of the parents. In this case, the rights of one member of the family were ajudged superior to the interests of the whole: rights of individuals increased at the expense of the family unit.

Many Americans sensed doom in such postwar modifications of American family life. "Declining" moral standards and juvenile delinquency symbolized this danger, and a vast sociological literature sprang up to explain changes in behavior and morals. Alfred Kinsey's bestselling *Sexual Behavior in the Human Male*, published in January 1948, proved to be one of the most sensational of these works. Undertaken in 1940, Kinsey's questionnaire research into the sexual habits of American men attracted wide attention and comment in the press. It elicited stern jeremiads from conservative religious leaders, but celebrations from liberal psychologists, who delighted in Kinsey's frank approach. The report became the subject of intellectual round-table discussions, cocktail party witticisms, *New Yorker* cartoons, and a great deal of uninformed speculation. Based on 12,000 individual case histories, Kinsey and his fellow researchers concluded that sexual practices could be explained best by linking them to socioeconomic factors, race, age, occupation, and region. They found, for example, that upper-level economic groups tended to encourage kissing and masturbation but frowned on nonmarital intercourse. Lower-level economic groups were more prudish about kissing but did not worry terribly about nonmarital intercourse. Differences occurred in other groups with different taboos.

Most importantly, this relativistic approach to sexual practice challenged the notion of a single, prevailing moral standard for all Americans. Kinsey discussed every variety of sexual activity dispassionately. He categorized behavior by types of sexual outlets: self-stimulation, heterosexual petting or intercourse—including marital, premarital, and extramarital—and homosexual activities. Making no moral distinction between types, Kinsey seemed to define normality as a combination of normal and "abnormal" acts. He wrote, for example, that one-third of all American males had participated in serious homosexual activities at one time or another, but that this cast no doubt on their identity as heterosexuals. And, simply by reporting widespread extramarital practices, Kinsey appeared to be legitimizing them.

His second publication, *Sexual Behavior in American Women* (1953), again a best-seller, continued his exploration of the same rich but controversial vein. Widely discussed in the media and made the explicit subject of several Hollywood films, including *Two Plus Two*, these books invoked a wide debate about American sexual practices. They became the starting place for an attack on older standards of morality. Liberals cited Kinsey's works when challenging film and book censorship or when pushing for revocation of city and state blue laws. Sexual practices, they claimed, differed enormously from the unrealistic laws that were meant to control them.

Sexual liberalism aimed not just at debunking normality and accepted standards; it also pursued public sensuousness for profit. In October 1953, a young Chicago writer and cartoonist, Hugh Hefner, on a shoestring budget and the fortuitous acquisition of the rights to publish a nude photograph of movie star Marilyn Monroe, launched *Playboy*, a new men's magazine. An immediate success, the magazine combined carefully circumscribed pornography with sophisticated articles and stories. Hefner made a bunny in a tuxedo and the monthly centerfold nude, complete with rouged and powered breasts, the symbols of a new public sensuality.

By the 1960s, Hefner presided over a commercial empire of sex. *Playboy* reached a circulation of over 800,000 in 1959. By this time a celebrity, Hefner turned his private life into further entrepreneurial ventures. His renowned parties were telecast in 1959 as the *Playboy Penthouse Show*. In 1960, he opened the first Playboy Club in Chicago. And, from 1963 to 1966, he published the "Playboy Philosophy," attacking repression and Puritanism in American culture, in his magazine. Greeted initially with considerable outrage, *Playboy* had become so accepted by 1976 that the future president, Jimmy Carter, confessed his private sexual fantasies in its pages without any serious damage to his candidacy.

☆ ☆ ☆

When critics began to reflect on American expectations about family life, they questioned the glorification of the housewife. Philip Wylie's 1942 diatribe, *Generation of Vipers*, anticipated later views of "Momism." Wylie blamed every social ill he could imagine on the frustrations of women trapped in the home. This misogynist handbook of epithets described women as raging, quarreling, murdering Cinderellas, responsible for civic corruption, smuggling, bribery, theft, and murder. Dr. Vincent A. Strecker repeated these charges in a more moderate guise in two books, *Their Mother's Sons*, published in 1951, and *Their Mother's Daughters*, published in 1956 with Vincent T. Lathbury. Here too, the authors blamed a variety of ills on the "life-wrecking crew of wives."

These pictures of enraged women trapped in unrewarding marriages constituted a small part of the criticism of the family. Throughout the 1950s and into the 1960s, there were countless other bleak portrayals of the American family. Perhaps the finest writer to test the brittle metal of the postwar marriage ideal was John Updike. Almost all of Updike's novels dwelt upon sexual satisfaction, or lack of it, in marriage. *Couples*, a heralded novel published in 1968, explores the loveless marriages and casual sexual encounters of couples who possess children but have no family life. Husbands and wives are pretty much interchangeable. While they can find no real existence outside marriages, they find no salvation within their relationships either. Marriage appears as a customary but hollow institution, an impermanent interlude in the eternal struggle to achieve sexual conquest.

☆           ☆           ☆

The literature of the shattered family in the 1950s and 1960s was extensive, frank, and sometimes brutal. Its counterpart in describing the younger generation is almost as wide and foreboding. In fact, popular culture seemed to be obsessed with the problems of youth. From the film *The Bad Seed*, in which innocence and youth disguise a brutal murderer, to *Rebel Without a Cause*, to the ominous *Wild One*, starring Marlon Brando, Hollywood repeatedly examined the angry and destructive lives of young people.

Of all the teenage juvenile delinquency films, perhaps the most interesting is *Rebel Without a Cause*. In this enormously successful movie, James Dean portrays a middle-class boy whose arrival at a new high school triggers events that end in tragedy and death. The three main characters, all fated to participate in the final destruction, live in broken or misshapen families. In Dean's family, the mother dominates a passive father; in the second, the father is overbearing; in the third, the family scarcely exists, and the young man runs wild in search of love and security. These stereotyped broken families became a standard explanation for every variety of juvenile misbehavior. These truisms were repeated not just in popular culture, but even in political settings.

Many of the witnesses who appeared before the special Senate Judiciary Subcommittee set up to investigate juvenile delinquency in 1953 repeated the charge that the American family had bred a generation of young criminals. Under the leadership of Senator Robert C. Hendrickson, of New Jersey, and Senator Estes Kefauver, of Tennessee, the committee held extensive and widely publicized hearings during 1955 and 1956 exploring the causes of delinquency. The committee even subpoenaed the publishers of crime comic books and leading film and television producers to answer charges about the influence of media on young people. Although the committee generally supported the position of academics and social workers, who stressed the complexity of the issue, its hearings helped popularize the notion that the United States suffered from a tidal wave of delinquency. Sensationalized news reports of violent and brutal incidents involving teenage delinquents underscored this national concern.

Kefauver's own feelings about the causes of delinquency probably paralleled the reaction of most Americans: he blamed the American family. But recriminations did not end at the fireside. Parents tended to blame schools; the media portrayed parents as weak and vacillating and child-care institutions as callous and brutalizing. The Gallup poll, however, repeatedly found that most Americans blamed declining discipline and loose family ties for youthful misbehavior.

The misbehavior that shocked some observers expressed freedom to others. Jack Kerouac, whose novel *On the Road* appeared in 1957, portrayed the juvenile delinquent as a cultural hero. In a breathless, Whitmanesque style, Kerouac penned a *roman à clef*— a thinly disguised autobiographical description of the lives of his friends in New York and San Francisco. As the author sped back and forth across the country, he encountered the cultures of down-and-out Americans, the music of urban blacks, and the macho masculinity of the American working class. And, as Walt Whitman had done before him, Kerouac celebrated the vitality and energy of these people.

Writing in a more academic mode, Edgar Friedenberg, in his book *The Vanishing Adolescent* (1959), described young people as scapegoats for social institutions that had malfunctioned. The adolescent, he wrote, was an individual in conflict with society: no wonder his contempt for a "society which has *no purposes* [his italics] of its own, other than to insure domestic tranquility by suitable medication." Delinquent behavior, he continued, was the understandable response of people treated as a class with few rights or responsibilities. As for crusaders against delinquency, he noted, their lurid overreaction to the behavior of teenagers displayed unhealthy aggression.

By 1961, it was no longer fashionable to worry about wayward youth. Since the publication of Friedenberg's book, much had happened: John Kennedy was elected in a campaign stressing youth and activity, and children born of the baby boom had entered their teens. Exploited by burgeoning media and consumer industry and no longer feared so much as courted and solicited, young people, merely in terms of numbers, came of age socially. As sociologist Kenneth Keniston told a conference assembled in 1961 to discuss the challenge of youth culture: "The Rock'n'roller, the Joe College student, the juvenile delinquent, the beatnik, whatever their important differences, all form part of this general youth culture." By the early 1960s, seventeen-year-olds emerged as the largest single age group in the American population, and their weight and special interests helped to shape society for several years.

Of all the works to explore the demographic and cultural changes in the family—to slit the seamless web of successful marriage—none was so sharp or ruthless in its implications as the nonfiction best-seller *In Cold Blood*, written by Truman Capote in 1966. Stylistically, Capote's work made a significant contribution to the "New Journalism," a new technique pioneered by other writers, such as Norman Mailer and Tom Wolfe, stressing their own participation in the events they experienced or fictionalized. But notice came to Capote because he focused on a brutal and pointless murder. To the author, the Clutter family was the perfect American family—loving, happy, successful, and healthily dependent upon each other. Their murder by two desperate thieves, therefore, became all the more senseless and tragic. Yet, the author's exploration of his own undisguised tenderness and sympathy for the murderers implied values that deeply compromised the traditional family and heterosexual love. For all the tragedy of the situation, Capote seemed to repeat what other contemporary authors were saying: the American family was disappearing. If perhaps not murdered by society, it was doomed by the extreme pressures of modern life and changes in values.

☆                              ☆                              ☆

Obviously, the American family changed after World War II. It was pulled in several directions simultaneously, and it responded by changing in contradictory ways. As early as 1929, President Hoover's Committee on Recent Social Trends reported trouble: the American family was losing its functions; division was increasing. Yet, immediately after World War II, the family reflected new optimism, and marriage and birth rates rose sharply. Then, just as abruptly, the bottom fell out of the marriage boom in 1957 and 1958, and the indices of instability began a rapid increase.

Those who predicted the death of the American family or lamented the passing of the paternal, nuclear family based their judgments upon nostalgia for what had been. That the structure and internal relations of families altered after the war is certain. Divorce by the 1960s rapidly increased, but so did remarriage. Various experimental relationships and living arrangements became commonplace by the 1960s. While many of these contradicted traditional moral axioms, they retained family characteristics. That these alternatives might become permanent was suggested at the American Psychological Association's annual meeting in 1967. Papers presented to the conference formed a symposium on "Alternative Models for the American Family Structure." As the editor of the series remarked, America was still committed to the family, but within this broad allegiance, room existed for experimentation and change, from group marriages to Margaret Mead's suggested "two-step marriage," new living arrangements for elderly people, and serial marriages. The future form of family life would be determined in large measure by the economic and cultural forces that influenced this institution. And none of these were permanent.

# 4 In the Shadow of the Cold War

The new President in April 1945 was Harry S. Truman, a man elevated by ambition, force of personality, and circumstance to a position for which he had little preparation. A small, bespectacled, intellectual boy, Truman grew up in Independence, Missouri. His haunts were neighborhood fields, the First Presbyterian Church on Sundays, and the Independence Public Library during the week. So diligent a reader was he that he had finished all of the books in the library and his family Bible three times by the age of fourteen. His favorite reading matter was history, including Plutarch's *Lives*, the histories of ancient civilizations, and biographies of American presidents. These accounts of the lives of great men confirmed Truman's belief that political leadership means decisive activity. No belief could have better sustained a man who delighted in tough talk and the pugnacity of American politics.

As a boy, Truman's early jobs brought him in contact with farmers, small-town businessmen and speculators, and workers: the variegated and transient population of a state on the eastern reaches of the American frontier. After high school, he hired out to the Santa Fe Railroad as timekeeper, living occasionally in hobo camps along the Missouri River. Shortly afterward, he secured a job at the National Bank of Commerce in Kansas City. By 1906, however, he returned to the family farm, which he operated until the beginning of World War I.

For Truman, like many men of his generation, the war pushed him from one career into another. His stint in the National Guard began before the outbreak of hostilities, but active duty sent him to France. When he returned to Missouri after the war, he was thirty-five, just married, and looking for a new career. Truman first chose haberdashery, but when his clothing shop failed, he agreed to run for local political office. His first victory was as county judge, a position he won by running as a loyal member of the Pendergast machine, which controlled the state Democratic party. Launched on a political career, the only real question was how independent he would be of his dubious supporters.

Truman's service in state politics was competent and honest, but relatively undistinguished. So too was his career as a senator from Missouri. First elected in 1934, he worked hard for most New Deal legislation. A loyal party man representing the political center of the party, in 1944 he was an ideal compromise candidate for the vice-presidency. Both labor and the South, the two largest contending forces in the Democratic party, agreed to him. These very qualities that made him acceptable, however, often worked to his disadvantage: the compromise candidate does not always become the best leader.

In many ways, Truman's presidency was accidental. He became a vice-presidential candidate in 1944, at a time when speculation had it that Roosevelt might not live through another full term. Yet, he was not chosen as a replacement, but rather as a substitute for an unacceptable replacement: Henry Wallace—then Roosevelt's vice-president, but *persona non grata* to the conservative wing of the Democratic party. Truman in 1944 was relatively unknown to the American public, except for his wartime investigations into defense-industry profiteering and inefficiency; he represented loyal but moderate support for the New Deal.

Truman's concept of the presidency combined the necessity of invention with guidance by traditional attitudes toward leadership culled from the biographies of great men and reinforced by his own experiences. To many who observed his career, he exemplified the American myth of success, a modern Horatio Alger, who through pluck and luck went from "window washer, bottle duster, floor scrubber in an Independence, Missouri, drugstore," to President of the United States. Even to Truman, this was a story only half-believed, and in recounting his success, he always displayed a measure of incredulity. As he said the day after Roosevelt's death: "When they told me yesterday what had happened, I felt like the moon, the stars, and the planets had fallen on me."

A shrewd and tenacious political fighter, Truman dramatically changed the tone of presidential leadership. Almost self-consciously the opposite of F.D.R., Truman delighted in making decisions and taking responsibility—even for mistakes. The momentous choices he faced—to drop the atomic bomb on Hiroshima and Nagasaki, for example—simply went with the job, he felt, and he did not shrink from making them. For this, supporters celebrated him, and critics castigated him. In foreign and domestic affairs, Truman acted quickly and sometimes rashly. He brought an element of wit, enthusiasm, and toughness to his task, perhaps best exemplified by the motto on his desk: "The Buck Stops Here."

Truman did not discourage the popular view that his tastes and language represented those of ordinary Americans. Truman brought straightforwardness, activism, and simple answers to the increasingly complex questions of the day. He, his wife, and his daughter symbolized the success of the traditional American family, secure in its values and steadfast, despite the pressures of postwar society. Affecting gaudy shirts on vacation in Key West, Florida, the President enjoyed fishing, swimming, poker, and the rites of the Masonic Lodge, in which he was a leader. When his daughter Margaret launched a singing career with a marginal voice, Truman was as protective as any father might be. In December 1950, after a concert at Constitution Hall, one of Washington's leading music critics reported the unpleasant truth about Margaret's talents. Truman rushed off a retort that later found its way into the press: "Someday I hope to meet you. When that happens you'll need a new nose, a lot of beefsteak for black eyes, and perhaps a supporter below."

Following Roosevelt's death on April 12, 1945, Truman had to assert his own leadership and yet convince the nation that he would continue F.D.R.'s policies. Although he paid lip service to continuity, he did not go out of his way to court Roosevelt's advisers. Sometimes acrimoniously, as in the case of Henry Wallace and Interior Secretary Harold Ickes, and sometimes quietly, Roosevelt's key advisers quit or were eased out, and Truman replaced them with his own men. Within a few weeks of taking office, Truman replaced Attorney General Francis Biddle with conservative Texas politician Tom C. Clark. Lewis Schwellenbach replaced Frances Perkins, the only female member of the Cabinet, as Secretary of Labor. Clinton P. Anderson took over as Secretary of Agriculture from Claude R. Wickard. Other appointments followed in June: Robert Hannegan to Postmaster General, James F. Byrnes to Secretary of State, and then in July, Kentucky congressman Fred Vinson to the Treasury. Two of these original appointees, Clark and Vinson, later received Supreme Court appointments. Truman's choice of Byrnes as Secretary of State proved an unhap-

*President Harry Truman* (right) *and Secretary of State James F. Byrnes at the bow of the* U.S.S. Augusta, *en route to the Big Three meeting with Churchill and Stalin at Potsdam, Germany.* (Office of War Information, National Archives)

py choice. Too independent, and perhaps thinking it should be he sitting in the Oval Office, Byrnes was replaced in early 1947 by General George C. Marshall.

In July 1946, Truman named John Davidson Clark, Leon H. Keyserling, and Edwin G. Nourse to his new Council of Economic Advisers. Keyserling, particularly, became important in setting economic policy. An active New Dealer who had helped draft the National Labor Relations Act of 1935, Keyserling favored programs stimulating economic growth rather than those redistributing wealth. Guided by efficient use of federal instruments of fiscal management, the economy, he hoped, would grow steadily, with minimal inflation. Keyserling's general orientation became the unofficial economic policy of both Truman's and Eisenhower's administrations; prosperity would solve the nation's social problems.

Truman had his worst time with Henry Wallace. A difficult, morally upright man, Wallace well understood that his liberal reputation had cost him the vice-presidential nomination in 1944. Barely confirmed by the Senate as Secretary of Commerce in 1944, Wallace, nonetheless, used his office as if he had a mandate for leadership. In some sense, he did. In Truman's Cabinet, he represented a large bloc of liberal opinion that was quickly losing its voice in the administration. Particularly outraged by the President's hard line toward the Soviet Union, Wallace first appealed to Truman. In a letter on March 14, 1946, he advised the President to try economic cooperation with the Soviets as a means of avoiding the foreign policy stalemate quickly developing over Eastern Europe. While not conceding American positions, Wallace suggested understanding Russian difficulties and recognizing the "lack of realism in many of their [foreign policy] assumptions and conclusions which stand in the way of peaceful world cooperation."

The President, however, neither changed his policy nor appreciated unsolicited advice from his Secretary of Commerce. When Wallace spoke at Madison Square Garden on September 12, 1946, publicly criticizing American foreign policy, Truman had to act to appease both Secretary Byrnes, who threatened to resign, and the press, which demanded to know who was in charge of the State Department. On September 20, he replaced Wallace at the Commerce Department with Averell Harriman. By appointing one of the architects of United States Cold War policy, Truman signaled his determination to continue confronting the Russians. Thus, the only substantial voice opposing American foreign policy departed from the Cabinet. Wallace later assumed the editorship of the magazine *The New Republic* in order to continue his fight.

Truman's postwar dealings with problems of strikes and inflation revealed a similar natural conservative streak. Although in 1946 the President promised Congress to hold the line on wages and prices, his actions ultimately stimulated price rises and exacerbated labor relations. Not, of course, that it was entirely his own doing. Truman shared Congress's desire to dismantle controls quickly and return initiative to business.

The problems of inflation and a rash of prolonged strikes made development of a consistent policy difficult, but Truman reacted to events as much as he anticipated problems. For the period from V-J Day through 1946, Truman lifted controls, reapplied them, or suggested new ones in his effort to speed the return of private management and free collective bargaining.

Only two days after the end of the war, Truman modified controls over prices, wages, and materials. Then, in September 1945, he suggested a tax cut, which Congress enthusiastically passed in November. Both of these actions warmed the engines of inflation. At the same time, the President announced that the National War Labor Board would cease its activities as final arbiter of wage increases. He hoped that a forthcoming Labor-Management Conference, scheduled for November, would establish informal wage-and-price guidelines. The conference, held in Washington, failed, however, to achieve any real agreement, and Truman's hoped-for industrial statesmanship did not emerge.

Because of looser controls and abrupt downward revisions in hours and overtime—resulting in declining wages—unions in major industries struck for substantial increases. Well might they have thought this a good moment to flex their muscles. During the war, union membership had increased spectacularly from about 9 million in 1940 to about 14.5 million in 1945, or approximately 36 percent of nonagricultural employees. Membership peaked at a higher point in American history than at any other time, save a brief moment during the Korean War.

Industrial strife boiled over during the fall of 1945 in the oil industry and at General Motors. In all, there were 4,600 work stoppages during that year involving about 5 million workers. The next year continued the industrial wrangling as steelworkers walked off the job in January after industry rejected a wage settlement of 18.5 cents per hour endorsed by the federal government.

In April, the United Mine Workers went out, and in May, Truman seized the railroads to prevent a strike. In all, Truman seized and operated nine industries under powers granted by the War Labor Disputes Act, which remained in effect until June 1946. Although many of these strikes were defensive—to maintain wages and membership gained during the war—the vast industrial turmoil during reconversion created a hostile public attitude toward unions and eventually infuriated Truman. In May, responding to the proposed strike of two railway unions, the President hastily penned a speech denouncing "effete union leaders" and called for vigilante action against them. Fortunately, his adviser Clark Clifford removed most of the offending touches, and Truman kept his political balance.

In approaching price controls, especially on foods, Truman pursued a contradictory policy. Although regulatory acts remained in force six months beyond the war, the President only gave weak support to Chester Bowles, the director of the Office of Price Administration. He also permitted the steel and auto industries to raise prices in order to compensate for wage hikes. And, the President failed to secure legislation extending an effective OPA operation beyond June 30, 1946. Facing a withholding strike of meatpackers and farmers, and despite pleas by housewives for continued tough controls, Truman permitted the deregulation of food prices. On November 9, after heavy Democratic losses at the polls, Truman lifted remaining price controls. In the resulting inflation, food prices rose almost 30 percent in six months. From 1945 to 1947, retail prices of round steak increased by about 86 percent; bread rose 42 percent; and bacon increased about 89 percent. The general consumer price index rose about 24 percent in these two years, after moving up only 22 percent in the four years from 1941 to 1945.

Truman's inability to provide satisfactory leadership in price policy or calm the angry strikes of the winter of 1945–1946 reinforced a growing conservative trend that influenced the congressional elections of 1946. Only twice between 1945 and 1970—in 1946 and in 1952—did the Republicans capture a majority in either or both branches of Congress. In a sense, both these elections were referenda on the Truman administration, one in its initial stages and one at its close. From another perspective, the elections were less significant. Whether or not Republicans actual-

ly dominated, the election of conservatives to Congress had sty-
mied the New Deal since 1938, and frequently blocked Truman.

In 1946, many Republican congressmen had promised their constituencies to undo the New Deal, but the only major New Deal
legislation ever threatened were the laws that regulated labor
unions. Unpopular because of protracted strikes and the butt of an
extensive media campaign, labor unions were also reeling from
internal struggle. In particular, after a year or so of jockeying for
power within the CIO, anti-Communist unionists, led by Walter
Reuther, succeeded in convincing Philip Murray, President of the
CIO, to support expulsion of Communist-dominated unions from
the brotherhood. When this expulsion succeeded in 1946, eleven
unions with around 1 million members were forced out of the
organization. Although this move delighted liberals and conservatives alike, it did not earn much public approval for other union
activities. More subtly, this ideological housecleaning signaled a
less aggressive posture of industrial unionization. Invited in during
the 1930s, when their organizational skills could be put to work in
the steel industry, automobile industry, and others, the Communists were accounted a major obstacle by many unionists, who
hoped for continued peaceful collective bargaining in recently
organized industries.

At first dubious of Truman, despite the friendly attitude of his
Secretary of Labor, and put off by his hasty actions during strikes,
the AF of L and the CIO were encouraged when he vetoed the
Case Bill in June 1946. This bill, introduced by Representative
Francis Case, of South Dakota, cut seriously into the power of the
unions. Pushed through the House without hearings, the bill
would have created a tripartite Federal Mediation Board for
strikes involving interstate commerce and a required cooling-off
period after notification of a walkout.

But Truman's veto only obstructed the inevitable. In early 1947,
the new Republican Congress came to Washington determined to
pass some form of restrictive labor legislation. During the first four
months of the new Eightieth Congress, members introduced over
seventy labor policy bills, most of them directed at setting up
public machinery to settle strike disputes. Choosing among com-
peting bills fell largely to House and Senate Labor Committee
chairmen, Representative Fred A. Hartley, Jr., of New Jersey,
and Senator Robert A. Taft, of Ohio. Taft, in particular, emerged

from this legislative turmoil as a national conservative leader, a latter-day David slinging his barbs against the New Deal Goliath. Certainly no friend of unions, Taft did not always fit the conservative mold, and his stands on some social issues, like public housing, and his reluctance to involve the United States in Cold War adventures cast doubt on the purity of his credentials. On the issue of "excessive" union power, however, there was no mistaking the appropriateness of his nickname, "Mr. Republican."

Just as adamant on the other side were the AF of L and the CIO, who wanted no modification whatsoever of the gains made under the New Deal Wagner Act. Dubbing the Taft-Hartley proposal the "Slave Labor Bill," major unions campaigned against its passage. Nonetheless, the Republican congress, aided by southern Democratic conservatives and bolstered by antiunion public opinion and strong pressure from business organizations, pushed through the act in the spring of 1947.

The most important features of the Taft-Hartley Act outlawed the closed shop (whereby to work, an employee had first to join a union), outlayed secondary boycotts and jurisdictional strikes in violation of National Labor Relations Board decisions, outlawed welfare funds except where jointly administered by labor and management, and made unions suable in federal court for violation of contracts. It required unions to file an annual financial report with the Labor Department and their own memberships. Union officials had to sign a non-Communist affidavit annually or lose their rights under the act. Employers and employees could petition for decertification elections, and federal government employees were forbidden to strike. Two final features legalized "right-to-work" state laws, prohibiting compulsory membership in a union shop, and gave the president power to invoke an eighty-day cooling-off period during which labor would be compelled to return to work.

Passed by the Congress on June 9, 1947, the bill went to Truman for his signature; now, the focus of lobbying and pressure politics shifted to the White House. Most of the important administration agencies, like the Council of Economic Advisers, and the President's political advisers recommended a veto. On June 20, Truman sent his reply to Congress: a sharply worded rejection of the law on the grounds that it undid the rights of workers and created massive government interference in union and management activities. That evening, Senator Taft went on radio to rebut the President's reasoning. Congress enthusiastically seconded Taft and voted the next day to override the Presidential veto, 331 to 83 in the House and 68 to 25 in the Senate. Aided by crucial southern votes in both houses, the Republican majority in Congress reversed the most liberal provisions of New Deal labor legislation.

Neither side fully anticipated the effects of Taft-Hartley. Advocates of the bill were disappointed when union political activity did not decrease; on the contrary, labor organizations realized their vulnerability and firmed up their alliance with the Democratic party. The new act scarcely affected serious union problems, such as a lack of internal democracy and racketeering. And those who hoped to use the act as the opening wedge to dismantle the New Deal were sorely disappointed. But the legislation did bolster postwar conservatism in major American unions and increased their reluctance to enter serious organizing drives. Through the antiunion shield of right-to-work laws, it encouraged industrialization of the Sunbelt using nonunion labor.

Opponents of the act wrongly anticipated that it meant "slave labor." Nothing of the sort happened. Truman, despite his vociferous opposition, invoked the act several times during his administration. Once they realized they could not repeal the act, established unions learned to live comfortably with most of its features. In fact, the greatest effect of Taft-Hartley was probably political, for Truman's veto message cemented the coalition that helped elect him in 1948.

If Republicans saw Taft-Hartley as a first skirmish in their Armaggedon with the New Deal, Truman and his advisers, particularly Clark Clifford, recognized in the act a pretext to counterattack and to secure Truman's reelection in 1948. To win, the President had to reestablish the coalition that had disintegrated in November 1946. This required considerable skill, for conservative southern congressmen opposed civil rights action that might encourage black Democratic voters. On the liberal side was the Americans for Democratic Action, a group that fought to reestablish liberalism free from the tint of radicalism that had been brushed on the New Deal. Since early 1947, this organization, peopled by illustrious former New Dealers and anti-Communist liberals, had promoted the nomination of General Dwight Eisenhower or Supreme Court Justice William O. Douglas to replace Truman. Further left, a Henry Wallace candidacy threatened to siphon off millions of votes in crucial industrial states.

In late 1946, the Democratic party leadership and presidential advisers met to consider Truman's future. The resulting strategy, outlined in a memo drafted by Clark Clifford in late 1947, analyzed the upcoming election, predicting that the Republicans would nominate Thomas E. Dewey, Governor of New York. Clifford urged Truman to appeal to liberal voters, to court labor and urban constituencies, to create a militant progressive program, and then blame Congress for failing to enact his program. In particular, Truman needed the votes of union members and of black and Jewish Americans.

The President had already moved tentatively in this direction. Following the Republican tidal wave of 1946, he issued Executive Order #9008 creating a Civil Rights Committee headed by Charles E. Wilson, President of General Electric, to propose a general program of civil rights action. Dominated by liberals with ties to labor and organizations like the NAACP, the body was predisposed to recommend firm action on civil rights. In June 1947, Truman personally dramatized his support for civil rights by appearing before the NAACP, where he promised that the federal government would become a "friendly, vigilant defender" of the rights of all Americans.

When the Committee on Civil Rights delivered its report on October 29, 1947, it handed Truman more, perhaps, than he had bargained for. The message demanded equality for all Americans. Besides invoking this respectable platitude, the report suggested concrete measures: self-determination for Washington, D.C. (a largely black city, then ruled by congressional committee), an immediate end to segregation in the armed forces, protective legislation for voters in national primaries (which in the one-party southern states were more important than elections), establishment of a permanent commission on civil rights, a stronger civil rights section in the Justice Department, and an end to restrictive housing covenants and discrimination in hiring and interstate commerce.

The President incorporated some of these suggestions in his civil rights message to Congress on February 2, 1948. When Southerners vehemently opposed such legislation and threatened to bolt the party, Truman beat a strategic retreat into inaction. In March, however, under pressure from the NAACP, other black organizations, and the Committee Against Jim Crow [segregation] in Military Service and Training, which threatened civil disobedience if the army were not integrated, Truman adopted Clark Clifford's